The Sweet Uses of Adversity: Images of the Biblical Job

Stephen Vicchio
&
Lucinda Dukes Edinberg

The Elizabeth Myers Mitchell Gallery
St. John's College
August 21 – November 2, 2002

The Sweet Uses of Adversity:
Images of the Biblical Job

The Elizabeth Myers Mitchell Gallery
St. John's College, Annapolis
August 21 – November 2, 2002

Exhibition Catalogue by
Stephen Vicchio and Lucinda Dukes Edinberg

Catalogue essay edited by Beth Schulman

Catalogue design by Cynthia A. Merrifield,
Merrifield Graphics & Publishing Service, Inc.

Printed by Baltimore Color Plate, Inc.

Cover illustration:
Ben Shahn, *Where Wast Thou?*
Amon Carter Museum, Fort Worth, Texas

IPP Press
The Institute for Public Philosophy
College of Notre Dame of Maryland
4701 N. Charles Street
Baltimore, Maryland 21210

© 2002 Stephen Vicchio and Lucinda Dukes Edinberg

All rights reserved. No part of this book may be reproduced or transmitted in any form or by any means, electronic or mechanical, including photocopying, recording, or by any information storage and retrieval system without written permission from the publisher.

Printed and bound in the United States of America

First Edition, First Printing

ISBN 0-9713748-2-1

ii

to Robert Gordis
who told me 33 years ago to learn Hebrew
and find time to read the Book of Job,
over and over again.
Stephen Vicchio

and

to Hydee Schaller
loyal friend, patient confidant
Lucinda Dukes Edinberg

Preface

> Each reader creates a Job in his own image. Throughout the ages, the unsophisticated believer and the recondite philosopher, the rationalist and the mystic, the skeptic and the existentialist, have all been fascinated by Job. Each has found in him something of his own temperament, some striking illumination of his own problems.
> Robert Gordis
> *The Book of God and Man*

> Ring the bell that still can ring,
> Forget your perfect offering.
> There is a crack in everything.
> That's how the light gets in.
> Leonard Cohen
> *Poems*

The biblical book of Job is not an easy read. The emotionally-charged dialogues between the patriarch and his supposed comforters are lengthy diatribes, often filled with heat, but not much light. The speakers in the dialogues talk past each other, any given speech rarely answering the specific claims made by the previous speaker. Job and his friends engage in long poetic outbursts, long lists of premises, followed by very few conclusions.

Its imposing length and turgid style not withstanding, the Book of Job nevertheless has commanded the attention of thoughtful people of faith for more than 2500 years. It was the favorite biblical book of Melville, Dostoyevski, and Kafka. In the seventeenth century it spawned a new literary form, the poetic biblical paraphrase. It was the subject of many non-canonical treatments in the ancient world, and some of the longest commentaries in the history of biblical scholarship.

For all the examining the book has undergone, it remains an enigma. Perhaps this is so because the issue central to the Job story is the problem of innocent suffering. In a world ruled by a benevolent and wise God, how could the innocent be made to undergo such suffering? In the case of the man from Uz, he does not simply suffer, he suffers on monumental proportions.

In this exhibit and the accompanying catalogue, we explore the many ways the figure of Job has been understood in Judaic, Christian, and Islamic culture. To put the matter another way, in this exhibit and catalogue we offer a series of snapshots. These snapshots are not so much of the Book of Job itself, as they are pictures of people looking at the Book of Job. The underlying assumption in this exhibit and catalogue is that what various peoples have had to say about the Book of Job over time may give us valuable insight into the various ways western culture has tried to come to grips with this fundamental issue: the problem of innocent suffering. In the wake of the events of September 11, 2001, there is, perhaps, no worthier topic to explore.

For this catalogue, I have written an essay that begins by exploring the nature of the received text. I suggest four major sources for understanding the inherent ambiguity of the Hebrew text of the Book of Job; unless otherwise noted, all translations are my own. I then go on to describe and discuss images of the biblical Job in western iconography, and to place these images within the historical and theological context of their time. My colleague Lucinda Edinberg has provided the text accompanying each of the images in the catalogue, where she speaks of their provenance, and some of the more important art-historical themes of these works.

Our interests and training are very different, and so we bring different perspectives to bear on the subject. I have been trained as a philosopher and theologian, and Ms. Edinberg as an art historian and educator. We hope this exhibit and catalogue are all the more rich for these differences. We also hope you find the exhibit and catalogue as interesting and as intellectually stimulating as we have found working on them to be.

Stephen Vicchio

Contents

Preface v

Acknowledgements vii

Part One: Essay by Stephen Vicchio 1
   The Composite Nature of the Text 1
   Problematic Portions of the Received Text 6
   Translation as Interpretation 12
   Nonbiblical Sources of the Job Image 18
   Some Conclusions About the Early Sources 27
   Images of the Biblical Job in Early Western Iconography ... 29
   Images of the Biblical Job in Modern Art 37
   Notes 43
   Bibliography 45

Part Two: Catalogue by Lucinda Dukes Edinberg 47
   Sources and Further Reading 100
   Artist Index 104

ACKNOWLEDGEMENTS

The Library of Congress: Katherine Blood, Curator of Fine Prints, for her help in image research and guidance.; Margaret Brown, Associate Registrar, who answered every question great and small cheerfully. We appreciate her expertise and the Herculean efforts facilitating the loans and photography from the Library of Congress.; Daniel DeSimone, Rare Books and Manuscripts Division for patiently retrieving many volumes to search for Job images.

The National Gallery of Art, Washington, D.C.: Peter Parshall, Curator of Old Master Prints, Virginia Clayton, Assistant Curator of Old Master Prints; Carlotta J. Owens, Assistant Curator, Department of Modern Prints and Drawings; Barbara A. Bernard, Department of Visual Services.

The Jewish Museum, New York: Juli Cho, Collections Manager; Irene Z. Schenck, Research Associate for her steady hand, constant look-out, enthusiasm, and scholarly advice from the beginning of this project. Barbara Treitel, Visual Resources Manager.

The New York Public Library: Robert Rainwater, Assistant Director of Prints & Photographs Research Library; Roseann Panebianco, Loan Administrator.

Amon Carter Museum of Art: Melissa G. Thompson, Registrar, for loan assistance and installation advice and Courtney DeAngelis, Associate Registrar.

Philadelphia Museum of Art: Innis H. Shoemaker, The Audrey and William H. Helfand Senior Curator of Prints, Drawings and Photographs; Ms. Ann Temkin, The Muriel and Philip Berman Curator of Modern and Contemporary Art; John Ittmann, Curator of Prints, Sally Malenka, Conservator of Decorative Arts and Sculpture; Amy P. Dowe, Registrar for Outgoing Loans; Nancy Wulbrecht, Former Registrar for Outgoing Loans, Stacey Bomento, Rights, Reproduction and Photographic Services, Gilbert Vicario, Curatorial Assistant, Ashley West, Intern.

The Kelly Collection of American Illustration: Richard Kelly for his generosity for the loan of a work from his collection, Elizabeth M. Alberding, Collections Manager.

Baltimore Museum of Art: Jay Fisher, Deputy Director of Curatorial Affairs and Senior Curator of Prints, Drawings and Photographs; Susan Dackerman, Curator Prints, Drawings & Photographs; Sarah Harman, Associate Registrar; Jennifer Sime, Prints, Drawing and Photographs; Beth Ryan, Rights and Reproductions Coordinator.

Syracuse University Art Collection: David L. Prince, Curator and Laura Wellner, Registrar.

The Walters Art Museum: Gary Vikan, Ph.D., Director, William Noel, Ph.D., Assistant Curator of Rare Books and Manuscripts; Laura Graziano, Registrar; Abigail B. Quandt, Conservator; Kate Lau, Photographic Services Coordinator.

Mrs. Lillian Ben-Zion for sharing her home and the works of her late husband, Ben-Zion; Tabita Shalem for sharing her knowledge and experience of the artist.

College of Notre Dame of Maryland: Catriona MacLeod, Ph.D., French and Latin translation; Suzanne Shipley, Ph.D., German text translation; Virgina Geiger, SSND; Therese Marie Dougherty, SSND; Josephine Treuschler and Margaret Steinhagen, Ph.D.

St. John's College: Christopher B. Nelson, President, St. John's College, Annapolis; Jeffrey A. Bishop, Vice-President; The Mitchell Gallery Faculty Advisory Committee, Thomas May, Chair; Hydee P. Schaller, Director; Sigrid Trumpy, Exhibits Preparator; Cordell Yee, Tutor and former Chair of The Mitchell Gallery Faculty Advisory Committee; Barbara Goyette, Director, Public Relations & Publications; Beth Schulman, Public Relations-Media Relations Manager; Suzanne Drucker, Graphic Designer; Kathleen Dulisse, Director of Community Programs; Harvey Flaumenhaft, Dean; Lisa Richmond, Librarian; Sidney Phipps, Superintendent of Buildings and Grounds; Paul Mikesell, Chief of Security; Tom Crouse, Manager of Technical Services; William Braithwaite, Tutor.

Cynthia Merrifield, long-time friend and Graphic Designer; Beth Schulman, editor.

Job Scholars: Robert Gordis, Marvin Pope, Nahum Glatzer, Bruce Zuckerman, Lawrence Besserman, and H. H. Rowley.

Friends and Family: Sandra, Reed and Jack Vicchio, Mary Lee and Tom Parsons, Sara Christine and Emily Edinberg, Laura Burns, Lois Milan, Jeff and Cathy Smith, John Popow, Roslyn Johnson, Joanne Jewett. Beth Wegner, Cindy Breloff, Dona Howard and Jude Johnston who were on board early in the project and took over the helm at home and in the classroom.

I.
The Composite Nature of the Text

> Sweet are the uses of adversity,
> Which like the toad, ugly and venomous,
> Wears yet a precious jewel in its head.
>
> William Shakespeare
> *As You Like It*

At the Holocaust museum in Israel, Yad Vashem, there is a sculpted piece by Nathan Rappaport. It is a solitary figure chiseled from cold stone: the biblical patriarch, Job. The man from Uz presses his fists to his chest, his eyes search the heavens looking for something that, at least in this moment, frozen in stone, has not yet come. Perhaps the most striking aspect of the sculpture is Job's ambiguous, almost nondescript clothing. The figure could be from the ancient patriarchal age; he might be wrapped in a medieval prayer shawl; or he could be clinging to a blanket hastily retrieved from a Krakow linen closet, before he was taken off to Auschwitz.[1]

Perhaps more than any other biblical figure, Job has stood as a holy, if sometimes ambiguous, personification of the extraordinary capacity of human beings to overcome overwhelming and often irrational suffering. Indeed, the biblical Job has served as a kind of metaphysical inkblot test, a sacred mirror if you will, in which the attitudes, hopes, and fears of Jews, Christians, and Moslems have been reflected over the centuries.

There are a number of reasons the biblical Book of Job has become the book of everyone who suffers. Some of those reasons are historical and theological, others have to do with the received text. Still others have to do with the way the book has been translated into Greek and Latin, and later into German by Martin Luther, and finally into English in the seventeenth century by the translators of the King James Version. In addition, particularly in the Christian tradition, the figure of Job has at times been more identified with noncanonical interpretations and commentaries on the text than with the actual Book of Job. These four elements—the difficulty and sometimes corrupted nature of the received Hebrew text, the composite nature of the text, the difficulties in translation, and the tremendous number of nonbiblical sources for interpreting the book—have all contributed to how religious people, throughout history, have made meaning out of the man from Uz and his book.

The most authoritative Hebrew texts of the book of Job have been inherited from two groups of remarkable medieval scholars, an eastern school at Sura in Babylon, and a western school at Tiberias, near the Sea of Galilee in Palestine.

These two groups of scholars—men who collectively became known as the Masoretes—conceived of their work as continuing and completing the earlier tradition of the *sopherim,* or scribal scholars. In addition to standardizing the consonantal sounds of the text, and adding signs for stresses and dramatic pauses for public readings, they also provided chapter headings and commentaries. Perhaps their most important job, however, was the counting of verses, words, and even single letters, so that the exact middle of the text could be ascertained. If a copied text did not have the same middle letter or word, then it was clear to the scholars that at least one error had been made in the transcription.[2]

Ancient Hebrew was written without vowels, often without spaces between words, and with no punctuation. By the ninth century C.E., another service the Masoretes had begun to render was the placing of diacritical marks to represent the vowel sounds, above or between the consonants, so that the texts might be read more easily. Eventually, the western style, the Tiberian method, became the standard one.

By the time the Masoretes had inherited these texts, however, there already were a number of scribal errors and anomalies present in the Book of Job. Indeed, the Book of Job is, quite likely, the most textually corrupted work in the Hebrew Bible. In more than a few places in the text, words seem to be missing, or are out of order. In other places, whole speeches are quite likely misplaced. One of the most significant facts of Jobean interpretation is that these errors and anomalies often come at pivotal points in the text. And these glitches were already imbedded in the texts received by the Masoretes.

The difficulty of the received text, coupled with the vastly different theological and philosophical assumptions readers through the ages have brought to the Book of Job, have made the tale of the man from Uz, an ambiguous, multifaceted, and sometimes contradictory exploration of the meaning of suffering in western religion.

The difficulties with the received text, and the very different fundamental assumptions one might bring to the text, have conspired with a third element to render interpreting the biblical Book of Job a difficult task, indeed. This third element consists in the fact that our contemporary book of Job is most likely the product of two distinct sources: a prose folktale (chapters 1 and 2 and 42:7-18) and the poetic body of the text (chapter 3 to 42:6).

These two fundamentally different sources for the Book of Job have led in the west to two very different ways of reading the book: one view in the prose narrative that emphasizes the patience of Job, and another view in the poetic dialogues that favors his *Sturm und Drang.* The Job of the prose suggests that if we accept good from God we ought also to accept evil, while the man from Uz depicted in the poetry is a Promethean hero who rails against the inequities of innocent suffering. The "patient" Job of the prose has tended to dominate the imaginations of artists and interpreters who produced the very first Jewish commentaries and psuedepigraphical works on the biblical book, as well as those in Christianity and Islam until the modern period. Beginning in the nineteenth century, however, Christian depictions of Job have more often stressed the solitary, existential view of the man from Uz, a "defiant" Job.

In the prologue and epilogue, Job is said to be "blameless and upright." He seems to have the complete approval of God, not only before his time of trial (1:1-3, 1:8, and 2:3) but also afterward (42: 7-10). The poetic portions of the text, in contrast, portray Job as a blasphemer, a doubter, and a rebel.

One important indication that the prose portions of the Book of Job came from a different original source than the poetic sections lies in the fact that the narrator in the prose prologue and epilogue uses the ancient name *Yahweh* when referring to the deity, while in the poetic portions of the text, Job and his friends refer to God as *El, Eloah, Shaddai,* and *Elohim,* but never as *Yahweh*. The prose narrator, unlike the poetic writer, was not moved by a theological prohibition that existed later in Judaism against using the ancient name.

These difficulties with the received text, as well as subsequent problems in translating the work, the vastly different theological and philosophical assumptions readers have brought to the text, and the realization that the Book of Job most likely comes from two very different original sources, all have conspired to make the man from Uz a most ambiguous figure. Some more modern commentators have suggested that Job remains defiant to the very end, while other more theologically orthodox scholars argue that the man from Uz learns that God has a divine plan that Job is only partially able to understand. Both kinds of interpreters find something substantial in the text to bolster their views, while at the same time often giving short shrift to portions of the text that do not fit neatly into their interpretive scheme. Throughout religious history, people have seen the "patient Job" or the "defiant Job," but rarely have individuals been able to see both.

In the same way that the composite text offers two very different views of the patriarch Job, it also offer two very different perspectives on God, one found in the prose, the other in the poetry. The God of the prose is anthropomorphic and a bit slow on the uptake. He enters into a bet with one of his heavenly creatures whose ontological status is pale compared to his own, but enter it he must. The God of the poetry is an imposing figure, so wise and mysterious that he speaks from a whirlwind. The God of the poetry could not care less what one of his creatures, heavenly or mundane, believes about the man from Uz.

This tendency to see either the patient Job or the iconoclastic Job, and their very different concomitant views of God, presents us with a series of lenses through which the received text came to be understood. In a real way, paying careful attention to what people down through the ages have said the Book of Job means offers us, sometimes in pictures, a history of the West's attitudes toward the meaning and purposes of suffering.

The Basic Tale

> There once was a man named Job who lived in the land of Uz,
> and he was blameless and upright, fearing God and turning
> away from evil.
>
> The Book of Job (1:1)

The opening lines of the Book of Job introduce the reader to a man who is "blameless and upright, fearing God and turning away from evil." Thus he is happy in the midst of his family and property precisely because of his good moral character, according to the theology of the day. The story opens with the picture of an exalted patriarch, surrounded by his kin, exercising priestly functions like the conducting of sacrifices of burnt offerings for the expiation of the sins of his clan.

The scene shifts then to the heavenly court, where God and the Satan are engaged in a kind of bet about Job's moral rectitude. The accuser Satan secures from God permission to test the virtue of our upright hero. Consequently, all manner of evils befall the man from Uz, striking first his property, then his family, and finally his person. Through all of this, Job perseveres in his submission to the will of God, though his wife asks her husband to "curse God and die."

While sitting on an ashheap scraping his wounds, the patriarch is visited by three friends, Eliphaz, Bildad, and Zophar. To this point in the narrative, events have been described in prose, but when Job begins to lament his condition, he does so in poetry. His friends, who act as interlocutors throughout most of the rest of the tale, also respond in poetry.

What follows are three rounds of speeches, with each friend speaking in turn three times, followed by replies from Job. In the present form of the book the third cycle of speeches is incomplete, the final discourses of Bildad and Zophar apparently mixed with Job's final reply.

After initially providing a week's worth of comfort, Job's friends turn accusatory. For the most part they suggest that the man from Uz has committed some serious sins, or that his children have, so that the reason Job now suffers is as a form of retributive justice or deserved punishment for past transgressions. In each of the replies to his interlocutors, Job responds vehemently and often angrily that he has done nothing to deserve the suffering which has come his way.

Beginning in chapter 32, a new character, Elihu, is introduced. He appears to take up the theological discussion of the cause of Job's suffering begun by the other friends. Elihu is introduced in a four-line prose introduction, but then speaks in poetry as did Job and the other interlocutors. Elihu expresses himself in a series of monologues, most addressed to the man from Uz, but some to the other friends. Unlike the earlier speeches of the other comforters, however, Elihu seems to argue that Job's suffering comes not as punishment, but as a way of making him a better person.

Elihu fades out of the discussion at the end of chapter 37, and is followed by God himself, who enters center stage in chapter 38. God speaks out of a whirlwind. His words come in a forceful poetry that far surpasses, in quality and power of language, most of the rest of the work. The bulk of the speeches from the whirlwind comes as a series of ironic and rhetorical queries of Job—"Where were you when I laid the foundations of the earth?"— all for the seeming purpose of establishing the conclusion that "Whatever is under the whole of heaven is Mine." In the face of these speeches Job is reduced to silence at first, then stammers a few lines in humility and repentance for having questioned the purposes of God and his creation.

The prose narrative then resumes in an epilogue that features the restoration of the man from Uz. Job recovers his former property two-fold. God gives Job a new set of children, seven sons and three daughters to replace those he has lost. God promises the patriarch a long life (140 years), and Job is told he will die in the bosom of his progeny.

This simple sketch suggests six major components of the book: a prose prologue (chapters 1 and 2); a lengthy collection of poetic discourses by the three friends about the cause of Job's suffering and Job's responses to each (chapters 3 to 31); a series of poetic monologues by Elihu, a fourth friend (chapters 32-37); followed by the speeches of Yahweh and Job's final response (chapters 38 to 42:6); and finally, the prose epilogue (chapters 42:7-17). Modern biblical scholars have questioned the authenticity of certain portions of the text. The third cycle of the friends' speeches is incomplete and out of order; some argue that chapter 28, a poem to wisdom, was originally an independent creation, and that the Elihu speeches were a later interpolation.

However urgent these issues have been to the modern scholar, for over two millennia the non-specialist reader has seen the book as a dramatic unity, as forceful a treatment as there has ever been on the problem of undeserved suffering. It was the favorite book of the Bible for thinkers as diverse as Moses Maimonides and William Blake, but it has also served as a comfort and a lesson for any person who has tried to make sense of the role suffering plays in the meaning of their life.

II.
Problematic Portions of the Received Text

> To the biblical scholar, the Book of Job presents a host of exegetical enigmas, eliciting a number of differing theological treatments in recent years. The range is staggering. Job has been described as both a rich man's fantasy and as a manifesto for the oppressed. Various approaches to the text, from the historical-critical to the deconstructive, have served only to complicate matters.
>
> William P. Brown
> *Introducing Job: A Journey of Transformation*

Although the basic story line of the Book of Job can be told in a few pages, the Masoretic text, our earliest received manuscript of the book, presents the reader with a number of textual anomalies or theological difficulties. One of the great ironies of the Book of Job is that these difficulties in the received text often come at precisely those narrative portions when the worldview of the writers is about to be revealed. Another element of irony about these particular sections of Job is that the preconceptions of subsequent readers of the text often made it theologically impossible to see what is actually there—the original theological intentions of the writer(s) of the work.

The opening line of the text serves as a good illustration: "There once was a man named Job who lived in the land of Uz and he was blameless and upright, one who feared God and turned away from evil."

The book opens with a prose narrative that, without any violence to ancient sensibilities, could be called an omniscient narration. Whatever else might be said about the work, one thing is clear: the original writers of the text wished us to think of Job as an unusually moral man. Subsequent interpreters of the text, however, often have failed to accept this basic presupposition about the patriarch's goodness. Indeed, from early talmudic speculations to modern commentaries, writers and thinkers have often pointed to Job's subsequent iconoclasm in the poetic body of the text as evidence of some perceived flaw in his character.

A second problematical portion of the text is the identity of the Satan in 1:6 to 2:7. This exchange begins with the Lord reminding Satan of his blameless and upright servant, Job, and then the arrangement by Satan, with the Lord's permission, of a series of calamities that befall the patriarch's family and property. Throughout this first round of trials, Job remains steadfast. The Satan responds by suggesting that Job has remained resolute in his faith because the calamities have not actually struck his person. Then, with God's permission, Satan brings on a second round of ills that include Job's contracting sores from head to toe.

Throughout Jewish, Christian, and Islamic history, the Satan figure in the Book of Job has been identified with later theological formulations of the demonic found from the intertestamental period on (200 B.C.E. to 100 C.E.). Subsequent interpreters of the Book of Job have tended to identify the Satan as the archenemy of God. But there is very little evidence in the actual text that the ancient Jews of the sixth century B.C.E., the century of the final compilation of the Book of Job, had any understanding of a demonic force in opposition to the Lord.

The original role of the Satan figure in the Book of Job is that of an angel in good standing in the heavenly court. His special function is to operate as a kind of devil's advocate, asking tough questions about human beings who appear to be virtuous, but may not be. One way to understand this point is to look carefully at how the Satan is first identified in 1:6:

>One day the heavenly beings *(bene ha elohim)*
>came to present themselves to the Lord
>and the Satan also came among *(betok)* them.

The *bene ha elohim*, literally "the sons of God," is a phrase most often associated in the Hebrew Bible with angels. It is more or less equivalent to another Hebrew expression *seba hassamaim*, "the hosts of heaven." The identification of the Satan with these heavenly creatures is clear because of the use of the preposition *betok*, "among." The word *betok* in all its other uses in the Hebrew Bible is employed to designate a notable member among a larger class of beings. Genesis 23:10 and 42:5 provide good examples of the use of *betok* in ancient Hebrew. In 23:10 Ephraim, the king of the Hittites is described as being "among the Hittites." In 42:5, the sons of Israel are describes as being "among" the other starving peoples who have migrated to Egypt. In both cases, Ephraim and the sons of Israel are notable members of a larger class of people.

In the Book of Job the Satan appears among the sons of God, those heavenly beings, because he is one of them. His special task, and thus the use of the definite article *ha* "the," is to probe the moral virtue of ostensibly good people. In the Book of Job, the Satan is better understood as a job description than a demonic name. This view is borne out by subsequent uses of the word "Satan" elsewhere in the Hebrew biblical text, as well as the logic of the book itself. The Satan figure was originally a kind of narrative device, included in the text to move the plot along. Indeed, the figure is ultimately unimportant to the outcome of the book, and thus Satan does not reappear at the end of the tale.

Although the Satan figure may have been theologically insignificant to the writers of the Book of Job, subsequent artists and interpreters have exercised a fertile imagination in depicting the figure. Most of the graphic demonic representations of the Satan figure are to be found in Christian iconography from the tenth century on. Often these personifications of evil are accompanied by insinuations that Job's wife, a figure who utters only one line in the original, is in league with the Devil.

Job's unnamed wife appears only in 2:9. After Job's initial calamities, she asks: "Do you still hold fast to your integrity? Curse God and die." In the original Hebrew two things are unclear about the wife's short speech. First, does she herself hold fast to Job's integrity? Does she believe he remains a man of faith and integrity? Does Job's spouse want her husband to die because she wishes his suffering to end, or because she has given up on his integrity?

The second interesting element about the wife's speech is that the ancient Hebrew word for "curse" is also the word for "bless." Some scholars suggest the wife may be using a euphemism here, but her small oration remains textually ambiguous in the original. Indeed, the wife was such an ambiguous figure to Greek-speaking, third-century B.C.E. translators of the Hebrew text, the Septuagint, that these Alexandrian Jews put another nine verses into the wife's mouth, explicitly stating her steadfastness.

If the wife's speech presents two very different possibilities in the Hebrew, subsequent interpreters, particularly those in the Christian tradition, have often taken the wife's speech as a sign that she is a consort of the Devil. Indeed, in Christian iconography from the twelfth to the fourteenth century, the wife is most often depicted as a shrew or a handmaiden of Satan.

The introduction of Job's friends (Eliphaz, Bildad, and Zophar) in 2: 11-13 also presents us with a number of puzzles in the iconography of the Book of Job. The Hebrew text tells us that Eliphaz was a resident of Teman, an ancient word for Yemen; Bildad belonged to the tribe of Shuah, probably associated with Aramean nomads; and Zophar lived in Na'amah, possibly Djebel-el-Na'ameh in northwestern Arabia. Although none of these places of origin are explicitly Hebraic, Christian iconographers, particularly in the High Middle Ages, nonetheless often have depicted the friends as rabbis, complete with sallow faces and accusatory fingers pointed at the man from Uz.

The makers of the Septuagint, through a misreading of the Hebrew, translate the identity of the friends as "kings." Although originally produced by Jews in Alexandria, later the Septuagint would be adopted as the authoritative text by Greek-speaking Christians. Thus all subsequent depictions of the comforters in Greek manuscripts of Job from the tenth century on show the patriarch's friends wearing crowns.

Chapter 19:25-27 also presents the interpreter with a number of vexing problems. Some Jewish interpreters, and many Christian thinkers, from very early on, have tended to see this section of chapter 19 as a confirmation of survival after death. It has been used in the Christian burial service for over a thousand years because of its supposed simple surety about the promise of resurrection.

A standard English translation of 19:25-27 looks like this:

> For I know that my Redeemer lives,
> and at the last he will stand upon the earth;
> and after my skin has been destroyed,
> then, without my flesh, I shall see God,
> whom I shall see on my side,
> and my eyes shall behold, and not another.
> My heart faints within me![3]

Christian commentators most often have seen this passage as an Old Testament precursor of Christ, as well as a proof text for survival after death. But to gain some sense of what this text meant for those who wrote it, we must look at two other places where Job calls for similar assistance.

In the first round of speeches Job longs for a *mokiah* or "arbiter" who might mediate between the divine and himself (9:32-33). A few chapters later, in the midst of harangues offered by his friends, Job asks for an *edh* or "witness" who is ready to testify on his behalf. Finally, in 19:25 this longing become a desire for an avenger *(goel)*, a kinsman in early Judaism who was duty-bound to see that justice was done for a member of his clan.

II Samuel 14:11 gives a good indication of how the term *goel* was understood by the writers of the Book of Job:

> Then she said, "Pray let the king invoke the
> Lord your God, that the avenger of blood (the *goel*)
> slay no more, and my son not be
> destroyed.

In this passage a woman wishes to spare her son from the revenge enacted by a *goel*, or "blood avenger." The Christian tradition, from early on, has translated *goel* as "Redeemer," leading to the Christological associations absent in the original text.

The other major difficulty with this passage is that the received text of 19:25-27 is hopelessly corrupted. Indeed, there appear to be a word or words missing from the text. As 19:25b stands in the Hebrew, it literally reads:

> That he the last will stand upon the earth.

This has led many translators to add "at" between the "he" and the "the." Whether this is a wise insertion, or whether it is the only possible insertion, have been matters of sometimes acrimonious debate. Verse 26 suffers from even more profound textual problems. As Samuel Terrien puts the matter, "Verse 26a is in a state of textual corruption which defies the resources of exegesis. The Hebrew of the Masoretic text is syntactically incoherent."

A literal reading of 19:26a gives us something like this:

> And after my skin they have peeled off (or mutilated)
> this she (or her).

Because of these profound textual problems, it is impossible to recover what the writers of Job meant by 19:25-27. That it is connected somehow to a belief in survival after death is highly unlikely. Indeed, a look at several places where the nature of death is discussed in the Book of Job should dissuade us from the suggestion that 19:25-27 is about resurrection of the body.

Direct references to the fate of the dead are made in 3:17-19, 7:21, 10:21-22, 14:7-12, 16:22, and 17:14-15, among a host of other places. From these passages one basic conclusion can be made. The major view of death to be found in the Book of Job is that death brings extinction, a ceasing to exist:

> Why do you not pardon my transgression
> and take away my iniquity?

> For now I shall lie in the earth;
> You will seek me, but I shall not be.[4]

One of the most interesting facts about the uses of the Book of Job in the western theological tradition is how often these three verses from chapter 19 have been appropriated as a proof text for survival after death. From the Septuagint to Handel's *Messiah,* the *goel* passage has been interpreted as a textual assurance of the life to come.

One final place worth mentioning in the Masoretic text of the Book of Job is 42:5-6, what many commentators have pointed to as the punch line of the work. In fact, of all the problematic passages of the Book of Job, the meaning of 42:5-6 has received the most attention from specialist and non-specialist alike. Most of the contention over 42:5-6 has centered on the best way to understand Job's response to God's voice out of the whirlwind. The condition of the received Hebrew text confounds the issue.

The Masoretic text presents us with four major textual difficulties in 42:6. The Revised Standard Version renders 42:6a this way:

> Therefore, I despise myself,
> and repent in dust and ashes.

The first difficulty in this verse involves the verb *emas,* rendered by the RSV as "despise." The word appears 18 times in the Hebrew Bible, and four other times in Job. If we examine these other uses we find that, in general, *emas* means "to reject," to "take back," or to "regard with little value." It rarely, if ever, means "despise" elsewhere in the text.

The second textual difficulty is that the Hebrew is not clear about what is being depised or rejected, for the direct object of 42:6a has dropped out of the Masoretic text. It therefore must be supplied by the translator. Some commentators have argued that *emas* is a reflexive verb and thus needs no direct object, but evidence elsewhere in the Hebrew text suggests otherwise.

Attempts at providing the missing direct object have been numerous in the history of translating and interpreting the book. The New English Bible suggests "all I have said," while the RSV adds "myself." Nearly all translations of the Book of Job take it for granted that Job is capitulating in 42:6, but it difficult to be clear about that simply by virtue of the received text.

Chapter 42:6b also presents two vexing textual difficulties. The verb *niham,* or with the preposition, *nihamti al,* means "to be comforted about" or "to repent in." *Niham* appears 26 other times in the Hebrew Bible, and eight other times in Job. In the other eight instances of its use in the Book of Job, it appears to be related to "comfort." A central question about 42:6b, then, is whether Job is "comforted about" the dust and ashes or "repenting in" dust and ashes. In the latter, the man from Uz would be piously accepting his fate now that he understands the superior wisdom of God, while in the former, Job might find it comforting that after he is dead, the Lord can no longer get to him.

It is rare in the history of translation that this rather impious latter translation is endorsed, but there is nothing about the original Hebrew text of Job that rules out this point of view. Indeed, in more modern times, where Job is often seen as a tragic hero, a Promethean figure railing against injustice, this translation is sometimes preferred.

We are presented, then, by an ancient puzzle in the received text of the Book of Job. In some portions of the puzzle we are required to rearrange the pieces to make sense of the picture. In other parts of the puzzle we must fill in the missing pieces to bring clear meaning to the text. All this must be accomplished with the understanding that the puzzle quite likely comes to us from two different manufacturers.

III.
Translation as Interpretation

> The translation gives us immense trouble on account of its exalted language, which seems to suffer even more, under our attempt to translate it, than Job did under the consolation of his friends, and thus, seems to prefer to lie among the ashes.
>
> Martin Luther
> Letter to Georg Spalatin
> February 23, 1524

The Septuagint Job

The Septuagint translation of the Book of Job was, for the first five centuries of Christianity, the major source for Christian views of the man from Uz. Christian believers living in the first 400 years of Christianity essentially viewed the book and its central character the way the earliest Greek translation did: as a patient sufferer who yearned to be vindicated through resurrection at the end of time. Although the Septuagint was originally completed for the use of Greek-speaking Jews in Alexandria, its popularity and influence lay mostly among early Christians. In fact, after the Septuagint version of the Old Testament was adopted by early Christian leaders of the Church as the authoritative text, it subsequently was rejected by Judaism as a less than reliable translation.[5]

The first element to notice about the Septuagint translation of Job is how short the text is: about 75% of the word count of the Masoretic texts. Curiously enough, in addition to the many omissions in the Greek Job, there are also materials to be found in the Septuagint that are not to be found in the Masoretic texts. Another major difference between the Hebrew and Greek texts are the latter's treatment of 19:25-27, 14:14, and the end of chapter 42.

The major differences between the Masoretic texts and the Septuagint are theological. Indeed, many of these theological differences were brought to the text, rather than occasioned by the text. Chapters 14:14 and 42:17 provide the clearest differences to be found between the Hebrew text and the early Greek version.

Chapter 14:14 exists in the Hebrew text as an interrogatory:

> If a man die, shall he live again? All the days of
> my service I shall wait, until my release comes.

In the Greek, 14:14 is rendered as a declaratory:

> For though a man may die, he will live again.
> All the days I shall wait, until I once again
> come into existence.

What is a bleak existential moment about the finitude of life in the Hebrew, in the Greek becomes a glorious and resounding vote for eternal life by the patriarch.

The Masoretic ending of the book is a terse, matter-of-fact recounting of Job's reward of extra life, 140 years rather than the biblically-prescribed 70 for a good man. The Septuagint, however, adds the following to 42:17:

> And it is written that he will rise again with those
> whom the Lord raises up. This man is explained
> from the Syriac book as living in the land of Ausis,
> on the borders of Edom and Arabia, formerly his
> name was Jobab.

The translators of the Greek text not only add the assurance of survival after death to the end of the text, they also attempt to solve the mystery of the location of the land of Uz. While the original shapers of the Hebrew text most likely wanted Uz to be "everyplace," as they wished his disease to be "the disease of all diseases," the translators of the Septuagint identify the patriarch with another like-sounding Hebrew name in Genesis, and place his residence on the border of Edom and the Arabian peninsula.

In general, the Greek translators tend to emphasize Job's moral character, his long-suffering patience and endurance. Many of his angriest speeches are muted in the Greek text. In the Septuagint, Job's piety demands he give way to the superior goodness, power, and intelligence of God. Chapter 16:13-14 offers another example of the theological propensities of the translators of the Greek Job. In the Hebrew text, Job speaks of God's visitations of suffering on the patriarch as "arrows" and Job as the "target," while the Greek text takes God out of these verses. They also change the singular pronouns to plural, so that God is not the killer of Job's children. Similarly, in the Hebrew the writers unselfconsciously announce that Job's sheep are killed in 1:6 by the "fire of God," while the Greek simply renders it "fire."

We have spoken briefly about the additions to 42:17 made by the Greek translators regarding Job's survival after death and his nationality. They also made another rather large addition to the text regarding Job's wife. We will recall that in the Masoretic text, the wife utters only one line:

> Do you still hold fast to your integrity?
> Curse God and die.

We suggested earlier on that the Job's wife is an ambiguous figure in the Hebrew. She may love her husband too much, and thus wishes to see him put out of his misery; or she may love her husband too little, and hopes he drops dead. The authors of the Septuagint offer a considerably less ambiguous view of the wife. In fact, in the Greek text, the wife's speech continues for another several verses:

> When much time had passed, his wife said to him,
> "How long will you hold out saying, "behold I wait
> yet a little while, expecting the hope of my deliver-
> ance?" For behold your memory is abolished from the
> earth, and your sons and daughters, the pangs and
> pain of my womb, which I bore in vain with sorrow,
> are all gone. And you yourself are seated among the
> corruption of worms, spending the night in the open
> air, and I am a servant and wanderer from place to
> place and house to house, waiting for the setting sun,
> that I might rest from my labors and my pangs which
> now beset me; but say something against God and die.

In the Septuagint, the wife is more of a person rather than simply a literary device as she is in the Hebrew. She voices a concern about Job's suffering, and also about her own. Indeed, she has been reduced, through the course of her husband's misfortunes, to the level of itinerant domestic, a far way to fall from the royal status the Greek text bestowed on Job and his friends, Bildad, Eliphaz, and Zophar.

Jerome's Job

Before the High Middle Ages, Christianity produced only one great translation of the biblical text, the Latin Vulgate of Jerome, who lived 346-420. When Jerome's tranlation emerged at the end of the fifth century, it replaced the Septuagint as the preferred text in western Christianity, and held that position for the next thousand years.[6]

We know from the examination of his letters that Jerome made two different translations of the Book of Job. The first was made from the Septuagint, sometime around 390. Dissatisfied with this earlier effort, Jerome began to study Hebrew with a rabbi, completing a translation from the Hebrew text about five years later.

Although Jerome points out in the preface to Job that he has striven to be faithful to the Hebrew, it is clear that he did not free himself from the influence of the Septuagint, nor from certain philosophical and theological assumptions he brought to the text. Because of his belief in original sin, for example, he suggests that Job is not "blameless and upright," as the Hebrew has it, but rather "simple and upright."

Jerome's translation of 19:25-27 also offers some insight into the worldview that informs his work. Earlier we took note of the many reasons that modern biblical scholars have been moved to remark that this passage is incomprehensible in the Hebrew texts we have inherited. Despite the textual difficulties, Jerome renders it this way:

> For I know that my Redeemer lives and on the last
> day I shall rise from the earth; and I shall be clothed
> again with my skin, and in my flesh I shall see God.

Jerome translates goel as "Redeemer," a word with definite Christian resonance, rather than the preferable "blood avenger" found in the Hebrew text. This led Gregory and many Christian commentators after him to see Job as a precursor of Christ, and as a harbinger of the resurrected life to come.

A third place where Jerome's worldview speaks boldly in his Vulgate translation are the many verses where the Hebrew text speaks anthropomorphically of God. Where the Septuagint translators in general chose to remove these passages from the text, shortening the text by about 25% overall, Jerome leaves them in, but softens them, eliminating any hint that God is not all-powerful, all-knowing, or all good. For its time, Jerome's translation was a monumental feat of scholarly perseverance, but one ultimately and substantially colored by his Christocentric monotheism.

Luther's Job

The great Reformation thinker Martin Luther completed a translation of the Book of Job in 1525. It is a more colloquial rendering than Jerome's translation, while staying quite close to the simplicity of the Hebrew grammatical constructions. In a letter written to Georg Spalatin on February 23, 1524, Luther gives some indication of how difficult he found the translation:

> The translation of Job gives us immense trouble on
> account of his exalted language, which seems to suffer
> even more, under our attempt to translate it, than Job
> did under the consolation of his friends, and thus,
> seems to prefer to lie among the ashes.[7]

Luther tells us in the preface to the translation what the purposes of the book are:

> The Book of Job deals with the question of whether
> misfortune comes from God even to the righteous. Job
> stands firm and contends that God torments even the
> righteous without cause other than this be to God's
> praise, as Christ testifies in John 9:3 when he speaks
> of the man born blind.[8]

Although Luther begins his preface with a rejection of traditional retributive justice, he nevertheless does not see Job as entirely blameless:

> To be sure, when Job is in danger of death, out of
> human weakness he talks too much against God, and
> in his suffering, sins. Nevertheless, Job insists that he
> has not deserved this suffering more than others have,
> which is, of course, true.[9]

Luther's conclusion to the preface is equally clear:

> So the book ultimately carries this conclusion. God
> alone is righteous, and yet one man may be more
> righteous than another, even in the sight of God.[10]

In Luther's view, no man is righteous before God because all men suffer from the stain of original sin. Thus he was led to the conclusion, as Jerome and Gregory were, that although Job was a saintly man, he was not a blameless one.

Luther was aware of the debate in ancient sources about Job's historicity. He explicitly mentions a number of ancient opinions on the matter. Luther argues that Job was an historical figure, but that the facts of the story may not have happened exactly as they are given to us. Indeed, he goes on to argue that the Book of Job would remain an inspired work even if the hero of the tale were a fictional character.

For the most part, Luther's translation is faithful to the received Hebrew text, though he does turn 19:25-27 into a pericope announcing the surety of resurrection at the end of time. He also gives a pious reading to 42:5-6, rendering it this way:

> Before I heard you with my ear, but now I have seen
> you with my eye, and thus, I despise myself, and
> repent in dust and ashes.[11]

Despite these many beliefs that Luther brought to the text, he was remarkable in letting the text speak for itself. Although Luther was a firm believer that the Satan of the Book of Job was a demonic force, for example, he managed to keep this theological assumption from bleeding over into the text. In many ways, Luther's translation was the first modern rendering of Job. He was careful in his philological work, and, for the most part, kept his assumptions about the text at bay.

The King James Version of Job

The Authorized Version (the King James Version) of the Book of Job, completed in 1611, is also an elegant and faithful rendering of the Hebrew text. Like all translations, however, certain important decisions had to be made about places in the original Hebrew where the text is unclear, or has obviously been corrupted. But there are, nevertheless, a number of places where the translators of the KJV have consciously chosen to depart from the received text. The King James rendering of 7:20 serves as an illustrative example. The Masoretic Version of 7:20 reads this way:

> If I have sinned, what do I do to you,
> watcher of men?
> Why have you made me your mark?
> Why have I become a burden to you?

In the Hebrew, the verse begins with the conditional "if," and ends with the direct object "you," and in between God is referred to as a "watcher of men." In the KJV, however, the verse reads like this:

> I have sinned; what shall I do unto Thee,
> O Thou preserver of men?

> Why hast Thou set me as a mark against Thee,
> so that I am a burden to myself?

In the Authorized Version the conditional "if" has been dropped, leaving "I have sinned." The "watcher of men" becomes the "preserver of men," and Job is no longer a burden to God, but rather a burden to himself. Again, the makers of the KJV reasoned that all men sin by virtue of the fact that they participate in Adam's original sin. The translators similarly relied on theological scruples and not the Hebrew when they changed "watcher of men" to "preserver of men," thus sidestepping any negative connotation the Hebrew phrase may have suggested about God. Finally, it must have occurred to the KJV translators that a perfect being could not be burdened by anything or anyone, and thus they make the patriarch a burden to himself.

Other theological and philosophical preconceptions the translators of the Authorized Version of the Book of Job brought to the text can be seen in the KJV's treatment of 5:1. The Masoretic text gives us this:

> Call out—who is there to answer you?
> To whom of the holy ones can you turn?

The King James translation renders the verse this way:

> Call now, if there be any that will answer thee;
> And to which of the saints wilt thou turn?

The KJV correctly identifies *kedosim* (holy ones) as plural. They are presumably the same celestial beings as those found in 4:18. But the English translators render kedosim as "saints." The original intent of the verse is to point out that no one can help Job. The KJV, however, begins with the Christian notion that the saints often can be of great service to the distressed souls living on earth. The Hebrew text asks a rhetorical question. The English translations answers that question with "the saints," a theological category alien to the makers of the Hebrew text.

Indeed, throughout the KJV rendering of Job, belief in soul/body dualism abounds. In 3:11, 13:14, 14:22, and 33:28-30, to name a few passages, the English text suggests that human beings are composite creatures, delicate combinations of mortal body and immortal soul, while in the Hebrew original, death is irrevocable and final. For the ancient Hebrews, consciousness ceases at death. In addition to these subtle references to soul/body dualism, the KJV also posits belief in resurrection at the end of time, rendering 19:25-26 this way:

> For I know that my Redeemer liveth, and that He
> shall stand at the latter day upon the earth;
> And though after my skin worms destroy this body,
> Yet in my flesh I shall see God.

Translating the Book of Job has never been an easy matter. The Masoretic text is filled with textual anomalies and disconcerting gaps. The difficulty in rendering the work from Hebrew to other languages, and the widely divergent worldviews brought to the text, have made translating the Book of Job a difficult and precarious enterprise.

IV.
Nonbiblical Sources of the Job Image

> Here it is sufficient to say that, as a commentary in the modern sense of the term, The *Magna Moralia* is well-nigh worthless. Gregory read the book in Latin. Of the original languages he knew nothing; of oriental manners and modes of thought he had no conception. He never seemed to realize that the book was a poem, or to have made the slightest allowance for poetic expression, images and metaphors. He understood it all with gross literalness. And yet, at the same time beneath the letter he fancied he discovered a wealth of esoteric meaning.
>
> F. H. Dudden
> *Gregory the Great: His Place in History and Thought*

As we have seen, the great translations of the Book of Job have influenced people's understanding of the figure of Job over time. The Septuagint in the third century B.C.E., Jerome's Vulgate translation in the fifth century, Luther's translation to German in the sixteenth century, and the King James Version in the early seventeenth century, all contributed significantly to Christian understandings of the text. But not all the philosophical and theological assumptions interpreters have brought to the Book of Job have come from canonical biblical sources, nor from direct translations of the text. In fact, in the Jewish, Christian, and Islamic traditions there have been a number of other major early sources about the man from Uz that are extracanonical. These sources, more than the biblical one, contributed to the theological and philosophical assumptions people over the ages have brought to the text.

In the Jewish tradition, by far the most important extracanonical sources for Job can be found in the apocryphal work, *The Testament of Job*, completed sometime around the first century B.C.E., and in early talmudic literature. In the Christian tradition, the most influential single source for the understanding of the plight of the man from Uz was Gregory the Great's *Moralia*. In the Moslem tradition, the Book of Job was primarily understood by way of the few references about the patriarch to be found in the Qu'ran.

The Testament of Job

The Greek word *apocrypha* (meaning "hidden" or "concealed") was used both by Hellenistic Jews and early Christian scholars to signify works of a biblical character that ought to be kept out of circulation for theological reasons, or to designate those texts whose provenance was unknown, and thus ought to be subject to more scrutiny. Any writings withdrawn from the public for theological reasons were either buried or stored in a secret place, the *genizah* (from the Hebrew verb *ganaz*, "to hoard"). King Hezakiah, for example, is said to have "stored up" the *Book of Remedies* because it ran counter to faith and trust in God. Thus, by the time of talmudic literature in the second and third centuries, the verb *ganaz* had come to mean "to declare as noncanonical." This notion of apocryphal as noncanonical was later adopted by early Christian scholars, including Origen and Didymus of Alexandria, both of whom made a distinction between "common, widely circulated books," and the "apocryphal" ones.[12]

The *Testament of Job* is a Jewish apocryphal work, probably written in Hebrew and appearing sometime in the first century B.C.E. One interesting clue to the origins of the *Testament of Job* is its frequent employment of the image of the patriarch as a "wrestler for God." This image becomes, later in Christian iconography, a ubiquitous one, but its sources are clearly Alexandrian. Philo, the first-century C.E. Alexandrian apologist for the Jewish faith, used this notion of becoming an athlete for godliness in his *Judaei de initio mundi* (The Jews at the beginning of the world). The writers of Second and Fourth Maccabees, as well, use this image frequently, suggesting the prize to be won in this contest of faithful endurance is the joys of resurrection. IV Maccabees 17: 15-16 makes this point quite explicitly:

> Reverence for God was a victor and gave the crown to
> its own athletes. Who did not admire the athlete of
> the divine legislation? Who were not amazed? [13]

Scholars generally agree that books II and IV of Maccabees are Alexandrian documents, written during the ruthless persecution of Anthiochus IV. This image of wrestler/athlete for God seems to have played a major role in galvanizing the Alexandrian Jewish community and giving them hope in the face of this persecution. The image of Job as athlete/wrestler is also a ubiquitous one in the *Testament of Job*. Indeed, the *Testament* goes well beyond the Septuagint in developing the figure of Job as an archetype for patience and perseverance, an athlete whose prize will be the joys of survival after death.

With this emphasis on the endurance of Job, the *Testament of Job* makes the patriarch privy to the bet between God and Satan, depicted here as a demonic deceiver. In fact, 3:4-5 of the *Testament* suggests that the holy Job is different from the rest of humanity in that he is not subject to Satan's deceptions. He sees the archenemy for what he is. Thus, the Job of the *Testament* is fully aware that Satan is the originator of his suffering, and that with patient endurance the prize of eternal life is to be achieved. For the writers of the *Testament* the major issue of the book was not theological knowledge (why God allows the innocent to suffer), but rather moral courage.

The wife's role in the *Testament* is also worth mentioning. As in the Septuagint translation, Job's spouse is given a name (Sitidos); she laments the death of her children in a speech lasting several verses; and, because of her husband's sickness, she is forced to work outside the home. Again, the prize to be gained by the wife in her faithful service to her husband is survival after death. The view of survival after death endorsed by the writers of the *Testament*, however, is not an easy matter to ascertain.

In chapter 39:5 of the *Testament*, Sitidos implores some soldiers to dig through the ruins of her collapsed house to recover the bodies of Job's dead children. However, in 39:9, Job declares that they have been "taken up into the heavens by their Creator, the King." Job tells those assembled to look to the eastern heavens, where they are given a vision of the children in their heavenly glory. Although these passages seem to suggest bodily resurrection, elsewhere in the *Testament* the narrator talks extensively about belief in the soul and its immortality. Philo and other Alexandrian Jews of the period seem to have believed in both forms of survival, as did the writers of Maccabees II and IV. Whatever view (s) of the possibility of existence after death are expressed in the Testament, one fact is entirely clear: the writers of the *Testament of Job* go far beyond the naturalistic understanding of death found in the Hebrew version of Job. The *Testament's* view also seems to go well beyond the earlier Alexandrian rendering of the Book of Job, the Septuagint, that argues for resurrection with no hint of immortality.

Job in the Talmud

The views of the patriarch Job to be found in ancient talmudic literature are strikingly different from early Alexandrian materials, both Jewish and Christian. Unlike early Christian sources from both East and West that seem indebted to the Septuagint/*Testament of Job* Alexandrian tradition, the ancient rabbinic thinkers of the Talmud, by and large, find the figure of Job to be much more ambiguous. While early Christian sources regard Job as a patient sufferer rewarded at the end of time with eternal life, the ancient rabbis' fascination with the man from Uz centers, for the most part, on four major questions: When did Job live? Was he a Jew? Was he an iconoclast or a patient sufferer? How are we to understand the causes of Job's suffering?[14]

Rabbinic opinions in the Talmud on the first question range from the era of the patriarchs around 2000 B.C.E. to the period of the late Persian empire in the second century B.C.E. One rabbi in *Baba Bathra* 15b ascribes authorship of the Book of Job to Moses. Other talmudic sources connect Job to Jethro and Balaam, who were consulted on the question of whether the Egyptians should exterminate the Israelites:

> When the Pharaoh wondered whether to exterminate
> the Jews, Jethro sided with letting Moses take the
> Israelites out and conveyed it to Pharaoh. Balaam
> opposed it. Job refused to take a position, wanting to
> remain neutral. It was for this neutrality that Job was
> later punished.[15]

Others rabbis of the Talmud said that Job was the grandson of Jacob's brother, Esau. After Job's testing in the book that bears his name, this source suggests he married Jacob's daughter Dinah. Over and against these opinions Rabbi Simon ben Laqish opined that "Job never existed. The purpose of the story is to serve as an allegory."

Ancient rabbinic views of Job's nationality are just as interesting, and every bit as contradictory. Many of the rabbis of the Talmud suggested that Job was not a Jew, while an equal number argue that he was among the most pious sons of Israel who ever lived.

The rabbis were equally divided on whether Job was iconoclastic or patient. Rabbi Nathan went so far as to suggest that Job was so holy a man that he put doors on all four sides of his house to better serve the poor who came for his alms. Over and against this view was that of Johanan ben Zakai who tells us:

> Job served the Omnipresent only out of fear, as it is
> stated in Job 1:8 "A wholehearted and upright man,
> one who fears God and shuns evil."[16]

Some ancient rabbis placed the man from Uz in the same moral company as Abraham, while others argued that Job's purported goodness came mainly from a desire for self-preservation.

By far the most extensive comments made about Job in the Talmud are in regard to the causes of the patriarch's suffering. Many of these opinions contradict the original premise of the Hebrew tale provided by the omniscient narrator in the opening line—that Job is blameless and upright. Indeed, the rabbis find various reasons why Job was not as morally worthy as the Hebrew texts suggests. One source argues that Job lived in the land of Canaan prior to the arrival of the Jews. When the scouts reported that the land was unoccupied, it was because the inhabitants of Canaan were all at Job's funeral. Job's troubles came early because God in his infinite wisdom knew that Job would die at the wrong time and ruin the report of the scouts, causing much loss of life when the Jews entered the promised land.

The Pesikta Rabba (190a) offers this explanation of the cause of Job's woes:

> Job was not like Adam who did not murmur after he
> was sentenced to death; he was not like Abraham who
> was told his seed would be slaves in Egypt... Had Job
> stood firm during his trials his name would be includ-
> ed in prayers, and men would call upon the "God of
> Job," as they now call upon the name of Abraham,
> Isaac and Jacob.[17]

Still other rabbinic sources suggest that Job's suffering came as a way of proving something to Satan about God's goodness, power, and intelligence. What all these comments about Job have in common is a passionate desire to make sense out of suffering. Some ancient rabbis made sense out of the patriarch's misfortunes by suggesting that they were deserved, while others held that Job's sufferings were part of a divine mystery that only the almighty was capable of unraveling. Thus, rather than answering the problem of innocent suffering posed in the original work, the rabbis changed the nature of the problem, or suggested that the answer went well beyond our abilities to comprehend it. Still, these rabbinic opinions about Job's national origins, his moral worthiness, and the reasons for his suffering took on a life of their own in the history of Judaism, often being quoted by subsequent Jewish thinkers like Saadia Gaon, Gersonides, Moses Maimonides, and others, as if they were authoritative answers to these questions.[18]

In addition to disagreements about these four major issues, rabbinic literature also abounds with smaller matters regarding the man from Uz. The rabbis often argue, for example, over whether Job's complaints are directed at God or at Satan. Other ancient Jewish scholars seem interested primarily in the nature of Elihu's moral character. Rabbi Akiba, for example, identifies the fourth comforter with Balaam, the reluctant traveler in Numbers 22. Akiba notes that God forgives the other three friends in the end of Job but says nothing of Elihu. Modern scholars usually argue that Elihu is not mentioned at the end of chapter 42 of the Book of Job because the fourth friend's speeches are essentially a precursor to those of God, and thus bring the same message of the divine plan as do the speeches from the whirlwind. This possibility did not occur to Akiba, nor apparently to the writers of the *Testament of Job*, who also see Elihu as a demonic deceiver.[19]

Job in Gregory the Great's *Moralia*

No other figure in early medieval Christianity in either the East or the West had the stature and religious authority of Gregory the Great. His *Moralia on Job*, completed at the end of the sixth century, remained the most authoritative Christian explication of the meaning and theological purposes of the Book of Job for 800 years. From the late sixth century to the fourteenth century, Gregory's view of the man from Uz became the normative Christian interpretation. This view was to define the history of Christian consciousness about notions of suffering in general, as well as particular understandings of the plight of the enigmatic patriarch from Uz.[20]

In the early Middle Ages, Gregory's exegetical insights on Job became synonymous with the Book of Job. Indeed, subsequent exegetical works on Job completed in western monasteries in the seventh to twelfth centuries are more often commentaries on Gregory's *Moralia* than on the biblical book itself. Of all Christian interpreters of the Book of Job, no one's influence has extended farther than that of Gregory.

Two facts bring Gregory's interpretation of Job into focus. First, the sixth-century bishop of Rome used a highly allegorical method of biblical interpretation. And second, Gregory shared a number of core theological beliefs with Jerome, Augustine, and other early fathers of the western church. These concepts included a belief in original sin and the fall of the human race, the idea of Satan as a demonic force, Job's wife as an agent of Satan, belief in both immortality of the soul and resurrection of the body, belief in a premundane fall of angels, and the moral culpability of the Jews for the death of Jesus.

After the time of Gregory these extratextual elements took on a kind of canonical status, due for the most part to Gregory's power and prestige and the new vision of the papacy he had managed to fashion.

Gregory tells us in the preface to the *Moralia* that the work was begun at the insistence of a group of monks at Constantinople who asked him to explain "all the mysteries that were concealed from them in the Book of Job." They urged Gregory "not only to bring out the allegorical meanings of the letter of the story, but also to give to those allegorical meanings the moral applications of which they were susceptible."

Gregory gives us a similar hint about his purposes in writing the *Moralia*:

> I desired to open the deep mysteries in the Book of
> Job, so far as the truth inspired me with the power to
> do so.[21]

The *Moralia* comes down to us in several volumes. Each verse of the Book of Job is discussed by Gregory in terms of first the literal, then the moral, and finally the allegorical level of the verse. For Gregory, this third level, the allegorical, was by far the deepest and most fruitful avenue of interpretation.

Gregory inherited from earlier church fathers the tendency to see Job as a patient, long-suffering saint. Indeed, he refers to the patriarch throughout the commentary as "Blessed Job." He saw the man from Uz as involved in a battle against the arch-deceiver, Satan. Like his predecessors Jerome and Augustine, Gregory used Job 14:14 as a proof text for original sin, suggesting that though Job was a good man he was not a blameless one. The sixth-century bishop of Rome was equally harsh on Job's wife. Gregory saw the wife as a mouthpiece of Satan. Satan speaks through the wife, he argued, when she tells the patriarch to "curse God and die."

Gregory saw the comforters Bildad, Eliphaz, and Zophar as stupid, mean-spirited men, and offered a fanciful etymology of their names to support his view. Throughout the *Moralia*, Gregory sees all four comforters as allegorical representations of the church's heretics, men too set in their own theological ways to be of any humane or theological service to Job, or yet worse in his view, as recalcitrant and meddling Jews.

In still other places of the Book of Job, Gregory finds allegorical references to the fate of the church and to the certainty of survival after death. One of the most creative of these comments is to be found in reference to 1:5, where Job makes sacrifices for his children in case they may have sinned in their hearts. Gregory suggests that Job made eight sacrifices. In the last one, he tells us, "Blessed Job was celebrating the mystery of the resurrection."

Gregory was also the first to find symbolic significance in the various animals described in chapters 39 and 40 of the Book of Job. Indeed, for Gregory, the Behemoth and Leviathan took on an extraordinary importance that they did not have in the original text. Gregory the Great saw the two mythological beasts described by the voice from the whirlwind as demonic creatures, representations of the power and cunning of the Devil. In fact, most eighth- to thirteenth-century depictions of Behemoth usually place a horned demon astride the back of the beast, while many of the representations of Leviathan from the same period depict the beast's mouth as the opening of Hell.

These themes of original sin, demonic activity, and survival after death have been discussed earlier in this essay, in relationship to the *Testament of Job*. But two other additional theological themes surface in the *Moralia* as well. The most ubiquitous of these is Gregory's tendency to use Job as a Christ figure. In nearly every verse that refers to the moral qualities of the man from Uz, Gregory likens these characteristics to the life of Christ.

The other new theme that Gregory introduces is his tendency to see various elements of the Book of Job as allegorical references to the moral culpability of the Jews in the death of Jesus. His treatment of 9:24 and 9:34 are typical examples of this approach.

In the Hebrew text, Job speaks in 9:24 about the unfairness of the ways of the world, how "the earth is given over to the hands of the wicked." Gregory suggests that the hands of the wicked are those of Satan "working through the crucifiers of Jesus, the Jews." Similarly, in the Hebrew text of 9:34 Job implores God to "take away his rod from me, and let not his terror make me afraid." Gregory sees the rod as the Jewish law, which was "removed by the incarnation." When Job sits on his dungheap in 2:8, Gregory interprets this as a symbolic representation of the incarnation, where the Redeemer takes on flesh to "suffer the pain of passion amidst the contempt of his people, the Jews." Indeed, in dozens of places in his commentary, Gregory identifies Bildad, Eliphaz, and Zophar, as Hebrews.

In these comments on Jews and Judaism, the quest for the deeper allegorical meaning of the text takes on a life of its own, as it does in Gregory's allegorical thoughts on demonic activity in human affairs, original sin, survival after death, and Job as a Christ figure. Even in passages where Gregory is ostensibly commenting on the literal meaning of the text, he often makes precisely the same sort of highly symbolic interpretations that he does when speaking of the allegorical meaning of a verse.

In a very real way, Christian interpretations of the Book of Job from the seventh to the fourteenth centuries became more or less equivalent to what Gregory had to say about the book. As Nahum Glatzer puts it:

> The success of the commentary was phenomenal… In the centuries following its publication, the *Magna Moralia* was many times translated from the Latin and epitomized, as well as read as a text book and compendium of Christian dogma and thought. The Book of Job proffered no message beyond the one the Gregory commentary saw in it.[22]

Job in the Qu'ran

At the same time that Gregory was preparing his massive commentary on the Book of Job in the early seventh century, Mohammed, a young Hashim bedouin of the Arabian Quraysh tribe, founded the syncretistic religion of Islam, the Arabic word for submission. A generation later, it had spread through all of Arabia. In the third generation it had become a world religion, spreading throughout the Middle East and North Africa. By the eighth century it had moved through the Iberian peninsula into Spain and Portugal.[23]

The record of Allah's revelation to Mohammed was recorded in the Qu'ran, which became a written text sometime after the founder's death in the mid-seventh century. There are two kinds of reference to the Book of Job in the Qu'ran. The first is a series of expressions and allusions that the writers of the Qu'ran either borrowed from the biblical Book of Job, or were so much a part of Semitic culture that they could be found in both the Bible and in sacred Islamic scripture.

As in ancient Jewish literature, various opinions were put forward in the medieval Islamic tradition about Job's origins and the period in which he lived, but the questions found among the ancient rabbis about whether Job loved God out of devotion or self-interested fear are never raised in the Moslem sources.

In addition to these linguistic and cultural parallels to early Jewish perspectives on Job, there are also a number of explicit references in the Qu'ran to the man from Uz. Each of the four major references to Job is relatively brief. In the first, 4:163, Job is referred to in connection with those worthies to whom Allah has given his revelation:

> We have sent thee inspiration, as We sent it to Noah
> and the Messengers after him: We sent inspiration to
> Abraham, Ishmail, Isaac, Jacob, and the tribes of
> Jesus, Job, Jonah, Aaron, and Solomon, and to David
> We gave the psalms.[24]

The second reference to Job in the Qu'ran comes in the context of patience as the ultimate counsel in regard to innocent suffering. Again in 6:84 Allah is the speaker:

> We gave him Isaac and Jacob, all three we guided.
> And before him We guided Noah, and among his
> progeny David, Solomon, Job, Joseph, Moses and
> Aaron. Those We reward those who do the good.[25]

The third mention of Job in the Qu'ran occurs in the context of questions about the proper attitude of good Moslems who are facing suffering:

> And remember Job who cried to his Lord, "Truly distress has seized me, but Thou art the Most Merciful of
> those who are merciful." So we listen to him. We
> removed the distress that was on him, and we restored
> his people to him, and doubled their number—as a
> grace from Ourselves, and a thing of commemoration,
> for all who will serve.[26]

Here again the premium is on fortitude and patience, which replaces the larger theological questions about why Allah would allow such worthies to suffer in the first place. The final mention of Job in the Qu'ran makes this point about patience even more explicitly:

> Commemorate our Servant Job.
> Behold he cried to his Lord:
> "The Evil One has afflicted me with distress and
> suffering."
>
> The command was given:
> "Strike with your foot:
> Here is water wherein to wash, cool and refreshing
> water to drink."
>
> And We gave him back his people, and doubled their
> number as a grace to Ourselves, and a thing for
> commemoration, for all who have understanding.[27]

The Qu'ran conceives of Job's suffering as a kind of test which he passes with flying colors. The source of Job's afflictions is not God, but the evil one Iblis or Shaytan. Indeed, nothing is said in the Qu'ran about Satan needing permission from God to bring woes to the man from Uz. All the emphasis on Job in the Qu'ran is on his fortitude and his ability to withstand the onslaughts of Iblis.

One of the most striking parallels between the Quran's view of Job and the *Testament of Job* is the manner by which Job is healed of his sickness. Whereas the Masoretic text leaves the process to our imaginations, the Islamic tradition and the *Testament of Job* make explicit reference to the healing of Job's sores through the flowing of a sacred stream.

This theme of Job's healing through a sacred stream was popular among medieval Moslem commentators. The most common Moslem depictions of Job in the eleventh to fifteenth centuries show the patriarch as a young man, wearing medieval Islamic dress. He is usually visited by the angel Jabrail (Gabriel), who often hands Job a flower. Between the two figures usually runs the sacred healing stream. Unlike Christian medieval artistic depictions of Job that invariably portray Job as a suffering man accompanied by his wife and friends, Islamic art usually shows a triumphant Job, a patriarch accompanied by a heavenly messenger and healed by the magic waters of Allah.

This association of Job with healing waters also gave rise in Islamic popular culture to a tradition of "Job's well" or "Job's stream," a kind of fountain of youth, which, according to legend, was variously located outside Jerusalem, in the Transjordan, in Hauran, and in or around Damascus. Indeed, from the late nineteenth century to the present, at least a dozen different locations have been suggested in Islamic literature for the location of this sacred stream, a feature that does not actually appear in the original Hebrew text of the Book of Job.

V.
Some Conclusions About the Early Sources

> In reviewing the major trends in the entire range of literature on the Book of Job, one cannot fail to notice that, with some notable exceptions, Jewish interpreters in the premodern period Judaized Job and Christian expositors Christianized him. Both sides, again with exceptions, avoided a direct confrontation with the text of the book, in order not to be exposed (or not to expose the pious reader) to the bluntness of the hero's speeches and the shattering self-revelation of God in His answer to Job.
>
> Nahum Glatzer
> *The Dimensions of Job*

Each of the four elements discussed in this essay (the composite nature of the text, its many textual difficulties, the difficulty of translating the text, and the many philosophical and theological assumptions interpreters brought to the text) have made the history of Jobean iconography rich in texture, variegated in form, and complicated in interpretation. Nevertheless, at least five general conclusions can be made about these sources to guide us in our interpretation of the enigmatic man from Uz.

First, although the Book of Job essentially presents two different men from Uz, the patient Job and the iconoclastic Job, rarely do interpreters of the text see both Jobs. Interpreters throughout the ages have tended to see Job as a patient and saintly harbinger of eternal life, or as a Promethean hero railing against inequity. In the former interpretation, Job's enemy is a demonic Satan, in the latter, an unknowable God. A simple corollary to this first point also holds: the biblical Book of Job offers two very different understandings of God, one in the poetry, the other in the prose. One image of God is stiff and theatrical, the other mysterious and profound.

The God of the prose is almost a cardboard character, quick to boast of his servant Job, and ready to allow his agent, Satan, to test the patriarch's character. The God of the poetry, on the other hand, is wholly other. This deity lambasts Job for his temerity in questioning his creation. The God of the prose is anthropomorphic, quick to react, easy to goad. The deity of the prose speaks directly from his royal throne. The God of the poetry is full of wisdom and power, so mysterious he speaks only indirectly from a whirlwind in the desert.

Second, from early on, the Christian iconography of Job has been primarily focused on the patient, suffering Job, usually surrounded by his accusing wife and friends. This tendency is due in large part to the Septuagint and *Testament of Job* traditions that generally stress Job's endurance and faithfulness. Indeed, the only reference to the man from Uz in the New Testament, in the Epistle of James, explicitly refers to Job as a patient man of fortitude.

In the Christian middle ages this emphasis on the patient Job was continued and supplemented with a host of theological ideas whose roots may be found in Gregory the Great's monumental commentary on the book, his *Moralia on Job* completed in the late sixth century. Among the ideas Gregory made synonymous with the man from Uz were belief in survival after death as a reward for his steadfastness; belief in original sin; Job as a Christ figure; the identification of Job's wife as a woman in league with Satan; and the identification of Bildad, Eliphaz, and Zophar with accusatory Jews, the killers of Christ. Gregory's allegorical interpretation of Job often allowed for a host of nonbiblically-based conclusions to be made by the Roman pontiff, conclusions sometimes at odds with the actual meaning of the text.

Third, while early Christian interpreters of Job were struck with the patriarch's steadfastness and moral courage, and with his vulnerability to demonic onslaughts brought on by Satan and his own wife, early rabbinic commentators, for the most part, were engaged by issues of Job's nationality, his moral virtue, and his place in the history of the patriarchs. Nowhere is the old adage about the Talmud more apt than in its discussions of the enigmatic Job: on any theological issues, any five rabbis of the Talmud will give you ten points of view on the matter at hand.

Fourth, very few early Jewish iconographic images of Job are to be found in the extant art of the West. This fact most probably stems from two different causes: the prohibition against graven images, and a lack of an univocal, canonical view of the meaning of the patriarch's life. While Christian sources tended to depict the suffering patient Job, early Jewish sources for the most part eschewed artistic representation because there was no single authoritative point of view about the book's meaning. The ancient rabbis were at odds about who Job was, and thus, what his life meant. Indeed, as early as the third century C.E., they even disagreed about whether the man from Uz was an historical person.

Finally, early Islamic iconography on the man from Uz tends toward the patient Job. All four major references to Job in the Qu'ran stress the importance of the patriarch's suffering as a test of his moral virtue, a contest he passes with flying colors and thus is duly rewarded. Consequently, Islamic depictions of the man from Uz almost always show us a restored Job, a man who, with the help of Jabrail, has done battle with Iblis and triumphed.

This Islamic view of Job again most probably has its roots in the *Testament of Job* tradition. Other elements the Qu'ran borrowed from the *Testament of Job* tradition include giving Job's spouse a name and a fuller identity, as well as a more theologically central role in the narrative, and the use of the dramatic device of the healing stream. While Christian medieval artistic renderings of Job portray him as a saint in the midst of his suffering, and early Jewish artists eschew any tendency to depict the man from Uz, Moslem interpreters invariably show us a triumphant Job, a righteous man healed by the sacred stream of Allah, the Most Merciful. At the height of its artistic flowering, Islam used only a small range of images to depict the dutiful patriarch. These images, brought to Islamic artists through the Qu'ran, could be found earlier in the *Testament of Job* tradition.

VI.

Images of the Biblical Job in Early Western Iconography

> In the course of the past twenty centuries, the Book of Job has been read as an expression of piety or, on the contrary, of religious revolt. Traditionalists among Jews and Christians told the ancient story in order to teach submission to the will of God in time of misfortune. Religious and secular humanists looked upon the hero as a Hebrew Prometheus.
>
> Samuel Terrien
> *The Iconography of Job Through the Centuries*

Job in the Earliest Artistic Renderings

The earliest Jewish representation of the Book of Job is to be found on the walls of the synagogue at Dura-Europos, a ruined Syrian city excavated by Franz Cumont in 1922 and later by M. Rostovtzev in 1928. This Hellenistic Jewish fresco, completed sometime in the mid-third century C.E., depicts the triumphant man from Uz, his belongings restored, along with his wife and Elihu. From early on, Hebraic representations of the man from Uz have tended to depict the restored Job, and not the suffering one.[28]

The earliest Christian depictions of Job are fourth-century Roman cemetery paintings. These twenty representations of Job (some now lost) usually depict a young Job, often without sores. In the cemetery at Domitilla, Job is a solitary seated figure. He looks as if he sits for a portrait that might hang over the family hearth. A similar image in the New Catacomb at Via Latina depicts a young and vigorous Job, his supportive wife framed in the background.[29]

These earliest images of the man from Uz, both Jewish and Christian, tend toward a restored Job, a man well rewarded for his patience and fortitude. A generation later, however, on the Roman tomb of Junius Bassus, a Christian and Roman prefect who erected a basilica on the Aventine in the early fourth century, we see a new Jobean development in Christian iconography. The inscription on Bassus's sarcophagus suggests the Roman statesman had been a recent convert at his death in 359.

The frieze of Bassus's sarcophagus consists of two panels, each containing five biblical scenes. In one of the panels Job is depicted along with his wife and Satan, who together tempt the patriarch to curse God and die. The wife holds her garment over her face, as if she were worried she might contract her husband's sickness. The Satan figure insinuates himself between Job and his spouse. This panel is placed next to one of Adam and Eve in the garden, along with a snake who slithers down a tree between the pair, tempting them to taste the forbidden fruit.[30]

The wife's concern for her own health became a major theme in subsequent early medieval western Christian art. A bas-relief of Job and his wife from an eighth-century sarcophagus in Arles, for example, represents a cautious wife of Job who pushes the patriarch's food toward him at the end of a stick.

The earliest Byzantine depictions of Job are different from Roman iconographic images of the same period in a number of important respects. Whereas the Roman depictions of Job and his wife suggest an alliance between Satan and Job's spouse, the Greek representations, in general, take a much more benign view of the wife. Secondly, early Latin manuscripts of the book often depict the three comforters as accusers of Job, while Greek representations, due to an error in translation, more often display the comforters as kings.

A number of tenth- to twelfth-century illustrations of Job appear in Greek cantinae, collections of paraphrases and reflections on biblical stories. These depictions tend to show the patriarch seated on his dungheap, surrounded by his benign wife and royal friends. A Byzantine psalter or book containing the Book of Psalms, completed around 1300 (cat. 1), repeats these same motifs.[31]

In the Roman church, following the time of Gregory the Great, the image of the "patient Job" was mixed with another theme found in the *Testament of Job*—"Job the Warrior." Rather than depicting Job on a dungheap, the patriarch is often shown in eighth- to eleventh-century texts as girding his loins, or preparing for an athletic contest or for battle.

In the *Testament*, an angel advises Job that

> You will be like a fighting athlete,
> Both enduring pains and winning the crown.

Job is shown in a number of Greek and Latin manuscripts from the period as a man who does holy battle against the demonic, either girding his loins or wearing a helmet and escorted by Patience. Two notable examples of this genre are the badly damaged *Job Girding His Loins*, in an eighth-century manuscript at the Monastery of Saint John, the Theologian, at Patmos, and a Greek manuscript from the tenth century owned by the Vatican Library. In the latter, Job, accompanied by the allegorical Patience, actually leads an army against the forces of Satan.

Gregory's penchant for understanding Behemoth and Leviathan as reifications of the Devil can also be found in various manuscripts from this period. One of the most impressive of these is the twelfth-century manuscript *Liber Floridus*, where a horned Devil rides astride an ox-like Behemoth. In the same illuminated text, the Antichrist is seated on the coiling tail of a dragon-like Leviathan. Another fine representative of this genre is *The Anti-Christ Riding Leviathan*, a twelfth-century illumination owned by the Bodleian Library. The dog-like Antichrist, teeth bared and astride a coiling snake of a Leviathan, does battle with an angel. On a stone pulpit slab from the thirteenth-century cathedral at Traetto-Minturo, Leviathan is also depicted as a coiled snake, but here its mouth doubles as the jaws of Hell. God's hand can be seen in the upper right portion of the piece. The divine hand drops a human soul into the mouth of the waiting beast.[32]

Job in Late Medieval Christian Art

A number of extant illuminated Bibles from the thirteen to the fourteenth centuries share many of these compositional features with earlier Christian depictions. Several late medieval Latin Bibles illustrate Job's speech with his wife in 2:9-10. In an illuminated manuscript from 1238, Job sits in the foreground, with his accusatory wife behind him. Job holds a scroll on which is inscribed his words in 2:10, while his wife holds a smaller scroll on which is printed the Latin text: "Are you still holding fast to your integrity? Curse God and die."[33]

This theme, repeated in several extant Latin manuscripts, was most likely intended as a damning of the wife with her own words. In one thirteenth-century Latin miniature, Job's wife holds a small scroll and is seated astride an ostrich; in chapter 39 of Job, the ostrich is depicted as a foolish and nasty bird who does not properly care for her young.[34]

In these illuminated manuscripts from the late Latin Middle Ages, Job's spouse is often depicted with a frown on her face, or pointing an accusatory finger at her husband. These illustrations eliminate the thorny ambiguity of Job's wife presented in the Hebrew text in favor of an image of the spouse as a temptress or consort of the Devil. One of the best texts for discerning this connection between Satan and Job's spouse is a mid-fourteenth-century representation of Job, his wife, and Satan, owned by the Musée Condé in Chantilly, France. Job sits on his dungheap. His wife stands to the left, actively berating her husband, while a cloven-hoofed demon beats Job with a cat-o'-nine-tails. The French subscript reads: "The devil beats Job with a stick, while his wife beats him with words."[35]

A northern Italian bible illustration owned by the Walters Art Museum (cat. 2) also takes up this theme of Job's wife in league with the Devil. Job sits on his dungheap, his body covered with red and blue sores. Up in the left corner a demon chomps through a support that holds up the Jobean tapestry, while the patriarch's wife points an accusatory finger at her husband. A similar rendering of this theme can be seen in a late twelfth-century illuminated French manuscript, the Sauvigny Bible. Job, covered with sores, is lambasted by three friends, all dressed as rabbis. A small demon in the lower left corner beats the patriarch's legs with a whip.[36]

Reflecting the worldview in Gregory the Great's *Moralia,* images from the late medieval period in the west also brought another new iconographic tendency—the depiction of Job's friends as meddling rabbis, often complete with sallow skin, sour expressions, and accusatory fingers aimed at the suffering patriarch. Illustrative examples of Job's comforters as meddling rabbis can be seen in Sauvigny Bible and an unidentified thirteenth-century Latin manuscript catalogued by the Princeton Index of Christian Art. A 1367 fresco by Bartolo di Fredi at the Basilica di S. Maria Assunta in Tuscany, also takes up the theme. A saintly Job, complete with sores and halo, is confronted by a single rabbi. A large, dark figure hovers behind the pointing Jew.[37]

In many other illuminated manuscripts from the period, there is no doubt left about the origins of Job's suffering. In an anonymous fourteenth-century manuscript owned by the Vatican Library the patriarch is seated on his dungheap, while Satan hovers above him, sprinkling pestilence. Off in the distance, another cloven-hoofed demon moves in Job's direction. Above the scene, at a more heavenly altitude sits Gregory the Great, surveying the contest between patriarch and demonic forces.

A French Book of Hours, completed some time in the second half of the fifteenth century and owned by the Library of Congress (cat. 3), contains an illumination of Job that includes a pointing rabbi accompanied by two friends in period dress. Job sits not on a dungheap, but on a bundle of wheat, yet to be threshed. The use of the wheat is a reference to the separation of wheat and chaff at the resurrection. Indeed, late medieval depictions of the man from Uz and his plight moved away from the demonic representations of the twelfth to fourteenth centuries, to more theologically hopeful images of Job. In addition to the wheat metaphor, artists of the period often painted castles off in the distance in their illuminations of Job. Again this reference is most certainly to the heavenly reward to come—a major theme in the Septuagint, the *Testament of Job,* and Gregory's commentary.[38]

The theme of a heavenly castle can be found in a host of illuminated French and Italian manuscripts from the fifteenth and sixteenth centuries. A mid-fifteenth-century book of hours illustrated by Jean Fouquet, and now owned by the Musée Condé, is a good representative of this tradition. A 1524 Book of Hours owned by the Library of Congress (cat. 5) displays this castle theme as well. A Christ-like Job with sores and white robe is attended to by his wife and friends. Unlike earlier medieval depictions of the spouse, Job's wife looks compassionate, as do his comforters.[39]

A mid-fifteenth-century illuminated Office of the Dead, completed by Jean Colombe, contains another typical depiction of the theme. A pious Job stands in his dungheap, the mire up to his waist. Four distinguished-looking comforters accompany the patriarch. In the right background can be seen Job's ruined property, while off in the distance, in the left of the composition, is the waiting castle. The entire piece is framed with ornate Gothic architectural elements, much of the detail made up of skeletons.[40]

A beautifully wrought late fifteenth-century French manuscript offers another castle image. A bearded Job with open sores sits on a dungheap, complete with refuse and bones sticking out of the pile. He is attended to by three benign comforters. One of the trio is about to touch the patriarch, a second folds his hands in prayer, while the third looks to the heavens. An impressive Romanesque castle looms in the background.[41]

As Job's friends and his wife gradually became more benign figures, two other theological themes began to emerge in the artistic vocabulary of Jobean iconography. The late fourteenth century brought the new images of Job as the patron saint of healing, as well as the patron saint of musicians.

In a German woodcut from the early fifteenth century Job is depicted covered with sores and seated on his dungheap as usual. But rather than being accompanied by his accusing friends, he is flanked by supplicants covered with similar lesions. Above Job's head is written: "Oh Saint Job." From the upper right corner extends the right hand of God. Literary interpretations from the same period sometimes represent Job as the patron saint of various diseases, including leprosy and syphilis.[42]

In addition to this allusion to the man from Uz as the patron saint of lepers and skin diseases, in the fifteenth century we also see the identification of Job as the patron saint of musicians. In Pierre de Nesson's *Neuf leçons de Job,* Job sits on his dungheap, but the comforters have been replaced by musicians. The music makers console the patriarch, who rewards them with a gold coins. Similar scenes are represented in dozens of French, Italian, and German fifteenth-century illuminated manuscripts, as well as various altarpieces from the period. Albrecht Dürer completed an altarpiece in 1503 on the same theme for the Cathedral at Cologne. The gold coins are most likely related to the *Testament of Job* tradition where Job turns his sores into coins to repay musicians for their kindness.[43]

The late fifteenth century saw the beginning of one more artistic theme in illustrating the man from Uz: the panoramic view of Job's calamities. Various artists in the fifteenth and sixteenth centuries, mostly in Germany, made woodcuts of the patriarch which feature a kind of story board. A fine example of this genre can be seen in a German woodcut from 1483, owned by the Library of Congress (cat. no. 4).[44]

In the left of the colorful woodcut Job is being consoled by his wife dressed in the garb of a fifteenth-century hausfrau. In the center of the piece, a bishop, a knight, and a peasant are on pilgrimage. In the right portion of the woodcut, Job's house can be seen collapsing in the distance. In the foreground various animals, including the ostrich from chapter 39 of the Book of Job, can be seen.

Job in Medieval Jewish and Islamic Art

One way to gauge the many differences among Christian, Jewish, and Islamic uses of Job in medieval art is to examine the few Hebrew illuminated manuscripts of Job extant from the period, as well as the slightly more plentiful Moslem renderings of Job in the eleventh to sixteenth centuries.

The Rothschild Manuscript, a fifteenth-century illuminated text of the Bible from northern Italy, serves as a good example of the preoccupations of Jewish illustrators of the period. The manuscript, now owned by the National Museum of Israel in Jerusalem, is part of a larger collection of works containing more than fifty secular and religious books from the period. Manuscript 180 depicts Job, with his restored riches, surrounded by his new sons and daughters. The scene occupies a full page, and shows agricultural and pastoral activities to which his new family members attend.[45]

Medieval representations of the man from Uz are rare in extant Hebrew manuscripts from the High Middle Ages. In the few works where the book is depicted, as in the Rothschild text, these illuminated manuscripts most often involve scenes of Job's restored state. Most of the stock images of the Book of Job prevalent in Christian art of the day, like Satan as a demonic force, or Job's wife as a consort of the devil, are absent from these Jewish representations.

Extant Islamic representations of Job also tend toward depiction of the patriarch's restored state. Following the Qu'ran's references to Job, Moslem illustrators of the High Middle Ages usually show the prophet Ayyub (Job) accompanied by the angel Jibrail (Gabriel) and ministered to by his faithful wife, Rahman. A Persian manuscript owned by The New York Public Library (cat.10) is a good illustrative example.[46]

A flowering tree stands in the middle of the sixteenth-century composition. Job, wearing a loincloth, is raised up by the angel, Jabrail, while a spring flows around the patriarch's feet. The waters wash away Job's afflictions. The angel holds a robe for the man from Uz, while his wife offers him a basin.

Another fine example of the Moslem tradition on Job can be seen in a fifteenth-century manuscript owned by the Chester Beatty Library in Dublin. The healed Job is accompanied by the angel Jibrail who presents the patriarch with a rose. The Arabic subscript reads: "Job was healed with the aid of these holy waters, and died at the age of 93." Several other Islamic commentaries mention this as the age of Job's death. The origin of this figure is unclear. It bears no resemblance to the considerably more robust 140 years given in the Masoretic text, nor to the 170 and 240 years mentioned in some manuscripts of the Septuagint.[47]

Islamic understandings of Job for the most part were derived from his treatment in the Qu'ran. There the patriarch is treated as a holy saint of extraordinary patience. Following the *Testament of Job* tradition, the Qu'ran mentions the man from Uz as a man healed by the waters of God, and amply rewarded for his suffering with the delights of eternal life.

As with Hebraic illuminated manuscripts of the period, Islamic representations of Job tend toward depictions of the restored patriarch. Unlike Christian texts of the period that portray the patriarch's spouse as a shrew, in Islamic interpretations Job's wife is shown as a helpmate, a woman who has made many sacrifices for her ailing husband.

In Jewish and Moslem representations of Job from the period, the patriarch is rarely shown with his friends. More often he is displayed, in both traditions, as a holy man whose fortunes have been restored because of his great fortitude.

Job in the Art of the Renaissance and Reformation

The Jobean panoramic view was also taken up by various Reformation and Counter-Reformation artists of the sixteenth century, again mostly in Germany and Holland. Hans Wechbelin offers a panoramic view of the travails of Job. The wife, dressed as a sixteenth century hausfrau, berates her bearded husband in the left half of the woodcut, while Job's livestock are carried away by thieves on the right. Behind Job and his shrewish wife the patriarch's house, on fire, appears about to collapse.[48]

Another sixteenth-century German panorama of Job, an anonymous work completed at mid-century, is a veritable compendium of earlier Christian traditions about Job. In the central portion of the woodcut, an emaciated Job, encrusted with sores, is beaten by an enormous demon. At the bottom left, two sore-covered supplicants pray to Saint Job. At the right, the musicians play, while the wife berates her husband. To the far right, Job's house collapses, fire leaping from the windows, while off in the distance, we see the castle of resurrection and new life.[49]

Hans Holbein the Elder completed a painting of a Jobean scene in the early sixteenth century. Later it became part of a *Icones historarium*, or history of sacred images. In this 1543 print owned by the Walters Art Museum (cat. 7), Job sits on his dungheap, berated by his wife who stands to his right. Behind them can be seen Job's collapsing house and various dead livestock. To the right, two of the comforters, dressed in sixteenth-century garb, gesture dismissively at the patriarch.[50]

Augustin Hirschvogel also offered a panoramic view of the woes of Job in an evocative work now owned by the National Gallery of Art (cat. 9). Hirschvogel offers a synopses of texts from Job and Proverbs, asserting only good comes from God. Included is destruction of Job's property and animals, and the death of his children.

Similar panoramic views are offered in various editions of Luther's Bible. In 1524, for example, Silvan Othman provided the woodcuts for Luther's newly completed translation of the Old Testament. Job sits on his dungheap, surrounded by his nagging wife and his accusing friends. In the background, Job's house has just fallen on his children, while bandits, dressed in late medieval battle armor, make off with his livestock.[51]

Nuremberg printmaker and religious iconoclast, Hans Sebald Beham also completed a number of woodcuts for an edition of Luther's Bible published in 1527 (cat. 8). Beham depicts Job on a mat conversing with his friends. Job's wife is in the background with her arms stretched out as if in distress at the plight of her husband. Above these earthly figures, God speaks out of the clouds the words aimed at the comforters from chapter 42: "Non estis loquutti coram me rectum sicut servus meus Hiob" (You have not spoken the truth like my servant Job).[52]

Artist and Counter-Reformation thinker Maarten van Heemskerck completed a highly allegorical rendering of Job in 1550 (cat. 11). This brown pen-and-ink drawing features a well-muscled and bearded patriarch astride a tortoise, a symbol of patience. Behind Job, trailing in his wake are the wife, three friends, and a demonic Satan who carries a whip in his right hand and kindling for a fire in his left. Job drags the four figures along with him, each attached to separate tethers the patriarch holds in his right hand. Another mid-sixteenth century Dutch engraver and fellow follower of Erasmus, Dirck Volkertz Coornhert, made an engraving after the Heemskerck image in 1559. The images in the Coornhert engraving were reversed in the printing process.[53]

Both the Heemskerck and the Coornhert depictions are illustrative of long-lasting themes in Christian iconography of the Book of Job: the emphasis on the demonic, the patriarch's wife identification as a consort of Satan, and Job's portrayal as a Christ figure. As in sixteenth-century German Protestant representations of the book, the destruction of Job's home and children can be seen off in the distance. But these Counter-Reformation thinkers differed from Protestants in that they reanimated the importance of belief in the demonic and its influences.[54]

One of the earliest Renaissance depictions of the man from Uz came from the brush of Baccia della Porta, later known as Fra Bartolommeo. His *Job: The Prophet*, completed at the very end of the fifteenth century, is a heroic composition. The patriarch, seated on a throne, is well-muscled and fully clothed. He holds a banner proclaiming "Ipse Erit Salvator Meus" (He will be my savior). Other Italian Renaissance renderings of Job can be found in the works of Lodovico Cardi and Girolamo Libri, who in 1505 depicted a Christ-like Job, along with Saint Sebastian and Saint Roch, patron saints of leprosy, martyrdom, and plague. Similarly, in Giovanni Bellini's *Pala di S. Giobbe*, completed at the end of the fifteenth century, a young Madonna and child are seated on the throne of wisdom. The pair is flanked by St. Francis and St. Job on the left and St. Dominic and St. Sebastian on the right. Both Job and Sebastian wear loincloths. They look as much like Christ himself as they do distinguished saints of the Church.[55]

Vittore Carpaccio's *Job and the Dead Christ*, a tempera on wood composition, was completed between 1505 and 1510. Job wears a loincloth and leans against a tree, which is half barren and half flowering. The dead Christ, serene and composed, lies on a marble slab covered with a burial shroud. The Job figure holds a walking stick in his right hand. The death of Christ is a sign of his own journey to restoration, if not in this life, then in the next.[56]

For the most part, Renaissance renderings of the man from Uz tend to the heroic and allegorical. Gone from the scene are Job's wife and friends. The themes of patience, endurance, and the rewards of the resurrection linger in these fifteenth- and sixteenth-century compositions, but they are highly allegorized. When the figure of Satan does appear in these Renaissance pieces he is often depicted as a well-muscled heroic figure, much like the man he is sent to torture. While sixteenth-century northern European depictions of Job often showed a panorama of the man from Uz's sufferings, southern Renaissance Europe, particularly Italian painters, displayed Job as a prophet of resurrection and a patron saint of the afflicted, themes explicitly borrowed from Gregory the Great but dramatically changed in their artistic representation.

VII.

Images of the Biblical Job in Modern Art

> In approaching the early modern and more recent interpretations of Job, the reader will note the strong shift from testimonies and adaptations rooted in tradition and doctrine to freer expressions of attitudes (even when they are based on the writer's intellectual stance rather than the evidence of the text), a greater variety of insights, a profounder appreciation of the human and artistic possibilities of the book.
>
> Nahum Glatzer
> *The Dimensions of Job*

The Heroic Job

Depictions of the man from Uz in European paintings from the seventeenth century tended to follow one of two themes. The first—Job as the patron saint of musicians—was a ubiquitous one in Germany, Holland, and France. The other—highly sentimentalized, Neoclassical, heroic representations of Job, picturing a well-muscled patriarch thoroughly harassed by his shrew of a wife, his nasty friends, and a host of out-sized demons—were more popular in southern Europe, particularly Italy.

The notion of Job as a patron saint of musicians reached its height of popularity in the seventeenth century in northern Europe. Peter Paul Rubens presented the Musicians Guild of Antwerp with his painting of Job in 1612. Rubens repeated the same theme in an altarpiece for the church of Saint Nicholas in Brussels. Dozens of paintings depicting Job as the patron saint of music survive in Germany, France, and Holland, including works by Bernard van Orley, Nicholas van der Horst, Jan Mandyn and Albrecht Glockenton Gaspard de Crayer.[57]

A number of sentimentalized heroic Jobs also survive from the seventeenth century. In Luis Giordano's *Job and His Comforters*, a nearly prone Job is pushed back by the harsh words of his friends, and balances precariously on a rock. Behind the three meddling friends, a dark, demonic figure seems to orchestrate the proceedings.[58]

Lucas Vorsterman, a member of the school of Rubens, also painted a sentimentalized Job after an earlier painting by his teacher. In the Vorsterman work (cat. 13), Job is surrounded by winged demons pulling at his garment and torturing him with a metal instrument. The well-muscled Job is nearly prone on a bed of wheat, his nasty wife tells him to curse God and die. The figures that populate Vorsterman's work are Neoclassical in style. His Job figure is classically heroic, like Milton's Samson.[59]

Near the end of the seventeenth century, Guiseppe Maria Mitelli produced an etching of the restored, heroic Job (cat. 14). The patriarch, in the midst of a celebration, is surrounded by his family and servants. The Job figure sits high on a throne, an unmistakable halo of sainthood around his head. The bearded figure looks far more like Christ, or an Athenian hero, than an ancient desert patriarch.[60]

One of the most beautiful and arresting of seventeenth-century artistic depictions of Job was Georges de la Tour's *Job Visited By His Wife*. For many years, a number of La Tour's paintings had been incorrectly attributed to other seventeenth-century artists. In 1915, German art historian Hermann Voss conclusively identified a substantial portion of the painter's work, including his Job. Jacques Thuiller, in an excellent discussion of the painting, describes it this way:

> It is unlike anything else we encounter in painting that century, and is surprising even in the context of La Tour's other works. La Tour transforms the wife into an enormous mass taking up two-thirds of the canvas, and has forced the figure to bend at the waist and neck to stay within the frame.[61]

Thuiller is certainly correct about the strangeness of the painting. It is as if La Tour has poured all the intense medieval preoccupation with Job's wife as an agent of the Devil into this one painting, so that the wife is seen as menacing and gigantic. This is especially striking when we compare La Tour's treatment of the wife with other contemporary paintings of Job and his spouse. Gaspare Travesi, for example, completed a *Job and His Wife*. In Travesi's painting the patriarch and his spouse are roughly equal size. Job stretches out his hand for assistance, while his wife draws away. There is no hint of foreboding in Travesi's painting, which depicts the wife as a shrew, not a supernatural or demonic figure.[62]

While these Neoclassical representations were popular in the mid to late seventeenth century, literary depictions of Job also saw the development of a new genre devoted to the woes of the man from Uz, the poetic paraphrase. These long poetic retellings of the Job tale, usually done in iambic pentameter, were popular in England, Spain, and France, and often accompanied Neoclassical depictions of the patriarch.[63]

There appears to have been very little interest in the biblical Job by painters of the eighteenth century. What attention was paid to the biblical figure was reminiscent of earlier periods. The century that Voltaire labeled "The Period of Optimism" has left behind few paintings of Job by major western European artists. One rendering of Job by Lattanzio Querena called *Job on His Ash Heap* is more similar to late medieval representations of Job than to his seventeenth-century predecessors. Other eighteenth-century painters who took up the Job theme included Johann Bergl, Giuli Lama, and Nicoli Grassi, but their compositions also harkened back to either the late medieval period or the Neoclassicism of the seventeenth century. For the most part, eighteenth-century painters seemed unmoved by the artistic possibilities of the Job narrative.[64]

Gerard René Le Vilain completed a print after the *Iob* of Fra Bartolommeo, sometime in the late eighteenth century (cat. 16). The enormous patriarch looks on from a throne, a reiteration of the earlier heroic Job of the century before.[65]

One curious representation of the Book of Job came at the very end of the eighteenth century. The title of the work gives exceedingly clear indications of its purposes. In typical late eighteenth-century style, it goes on nearly as long as Job's suffering: *A Curious Hieroglyphic Bible, or Select Passages in the Old and New Testaments, represented with emblematic figures, for the amusement of youth: designed chiefly to familiarize those of tender age, in a pleasing and diverting manner, with early ideas of the Holy Scripture to which are subjoined a short account of the lives of the Evangelists, and other pieces, illustrated with cuts.* (cat. 17).[66]

The Romantic Job

Interest in Job was revived by the romantics, particularly by William Blake's illustrations, completed in 1825 (cat. 18-23). The engravings were commissioned by John Linnell, a generous benefactor in Blake's later career. The Bible was long an interest of Blake's, particularly the Book of Job. Although Blake's illustrations of the entire Book of Job came at the end of his life, his interest in the enigmatic man from Uz was a lifelong one. In 1785, Blake completed a drawing of Job protesting his innocence. It was completely redone seven years later as a powerful sepia painting. A year after that, in 1793, he engraved the work with a line from Job's speeches to God: "What is man that He should try him at every moment?"[67]

After Blake's death in 1827, his renderings of the Book of Job were alternately seen as containing mystical secrets, as entirely baffling, or quite mistakenly, as conventionally pious depictions of the Old Testament patriarch. In 1915, an English group of Theosophists published a special version of tarot cards drawn to follow Blake's renderings of the Book of Job. It was not until the publication, in 1910, of Joseph Wicksteed's *Blake's Vision of the Book of Job* that a more sober understanding of Blake's purposes began to emerge.[68]

In the seventeenth century, Neoclassical writers like Milton and Donne had tied the patience of the biblical Job to classical writers of the Stoic tradition like Lucretius. Donne went so far as to proclaim that Job was the archetype for the Renaissance man, while Milton in his *Paradise Regained* and *Samson Agonistes* identified Job's virtues with those of Samson and other ancient and classical worthies.[69]

Among the romantics, the figure of Job was given a very different meaning. J.G. Herder, the great German romantic, tells us that Job does not simply have the patience of Lucretius, he far surpasses the Roman philosopher in moral character because he understands the importance of passion and the quest in making life meaningful. Indeed, the Job of the poetry, the Job of passion and defiance, is the one that attracted the attention of the romantics, whether it was Blake and Byron in England, Lamartine and Hugo in France, or Herder and Goethe in Germany.[70]

Other romantic artists, such as Paul Gustave Dore and Christian Ernst Stölzel, also produced romantic Jobs. Dore's engraving *Job* depicts the man from Uz as an Oriental patriarch holding forth from his ashheap with his three friends, all in Arabian dress. Stölzel's *Job* (cat. no. 24), an 1833 composition, also depicts a bearded and well-muscled Oriental Job accompanied by his three Arabian-clad friends. To the right, in the distance, Elihu approaches. Job's crumbling property can be seen in the background to the left. The middle comforter of the trio raises an index finger, as if making a theological point. The other two friends are contemplative, respectful of the suffering patriarch.[71]

Paul Falconer Poole also produced a highly allegorical, romantic version of the man from Uz in 1833, at the height of English romanticism. Herbert Bourne rendered the painting as an engraving sometime in the mid-nineteenth century (cat. 25). In Bourne's work, Job sits in an Oriental setting surrounded by his wife and friends. The messenger of chapter 1: 14-15 appears in the center of the engraving announcing the woes that have befallen Job's family and possessions. Job' wife, absorbing the news, clutches at her breast, while a winged Satan observes the scene.[72]

Between 1896 and 1902, James Tissot completed a series of works on the Jobean theme done in gouache on board (cat. nos. 27-31). Tissot, a spiritualist and self-described devout Catholic, produced this evocative series of Job in an Oriental setting, reminiscent of earlier romantic treatments of the man from Uz and his plight. But the biblical Job also gave Tissot an opportunity to render a theme that pre-occupied him for much of his artistic career: that the pleasures of the rich and wellborn are often fraught with a sadness and tension that the glittering surfaces cannot mask. The Jobean narrative is played out in the Tissot renderings against a background of elegant draperies and fine furniture; this seems to make the pain of the patriarch all the more palpable.[73]

The Existential Job

The latter half of the nineteenth century brought a new artistic perspective on the man from Uz. In paintings of the period, Job is often depicted as a solitary, existential hero. The portrait painter and professor of painting Alexandre Gabriel Decamps completed a version of *Job on the Ashheap* at the very end of the nineteenth century. Unlike seventeenth-century Dutch renderings where Job is a solitary but serene figure, a Stoic hero full of patience and fortitude, Decamps's Job is shown in pain and isolation.[74]

Franz Gruber's *Job* is another illustrative example of this "Existential Job." Gruber, a Viennese painter who died in 1862, renders Job as a solitary figure, framed in the background by squalid tenements. Job sits on a stool, his right leg crossed over his bony left knee. His weary head rests in his left hand. A discarded parchment lies on the earthen floor. The scene is one of dejection and despair. There is neither patience, nor iconoclasm here. The overall mood is one of hopelessness and exhaustion.[75]

A similar perspective was taken by Alphonse Legros in his rendering of the man from Uz (cat. 26). A solitary, bearded Job sits on a small hillock. Behind him is a partially destroyed wall. The patriarch's face is angst-ridden. His posture suggests despair and exhaustion. Legros's Job is not heroic. He appears worn out, defeated by something he does not understand.[76]

Francois Nermeylen's *Job Dejected*, a plaster sculpted piece completed around 1880 is another notable example of this "Existential Job" genre. Nermeylen's Job reflects a deep melancholy, so deep that it seems to seep into the bones of the seated, solitary figure. Nermeylen's Job is a man defeated by unknowable forces.[77]

Oskar Kokoschka, haunted by his experiences fighting for the Austro-Prussian army in World War I, produced an abstract expressionist lithograph to accompany a short three-scene play on Job he completed in 1917. Job, accompanied by his wife, is portrayed as a living corpse. Their bodies are intertwined in a dance of death. It is perhaps the most despondent Job to appear in western art prior to the period of the

Holocaust. Other existential Jobs include Max Liebermann's *Job* in cool, austere colors. The patriarch sits alone, surrounded by a bleak, unforgiving landscape, reminiscent of T.S. Eliot's wasteland, and Julo Levin's 1933 rendering of a solitary, brooding man from Uz.[78]

The Post-Holocaust Job

Very few explicitly Christian painters have turned to Job in the latter half of the twentieth century. The most notable exceptions are works produced by Otto Dix in 1946, Emil Wachter in 1982, and Ernest Fuchs in 1963. Fuchs's etching features an emaciated Job in the lower center of the picture. The man from Uz is dominated by an enormous, overpowering Satan, displaying an extraordinary wingspan, talons, and a serpent's tongue. The Satan hovers over the helpless Job whose skinny arms are raised in defense. This Fuchs etching is interesting because it mixes earlier themes we have seen in the medieval Christian tradition on Job with the more modern penchant to depict Job as a lonely, solitary figure.

The events of the Second World War, with its combat carnage, the bombing of major cities like Dresden, London, and Hiroshima, and the horrors of the Holocaust, brought a renewed interest in the Book of Job among Jewish artists of the second half of the twentieth century. In much post-Holocaust Jewish literature as well, the figure of Job was used as an archetypal representative of the innocent sufferer.

Ivan Mestrovic produced a bronze sculpted piece of Job completed in the final days of World War II (cat. 36). The Yugoslavian-born Mestrovic is best known for his monumental sculpture at Grant Park in Chicago. He was imprisoned several years in Hungary for sedition, and came to the United States in 1951, following his release. Mestrovic's Job is a solitary figure. His weary head slips between his knees. The patriarch's body seems to bend under the invisible assault. His hair is ragged and his clothes show weathering, as if he has been exposed to all manner of physical and mental torment.[79]

Fritz Eichenberg's wood engraving of Job (cat. 42) was one of ten engravings illustrating the Hebrew Bible/Old Testament for the *Catholic Worker*. Eichenberg left Germany to escape Hitler in 1933. He eventually moved to New York, where he worked for the Works Progress Administration. Perhaps not surprisingly, Eichenberg was a great admirer of Dostoyevski, Tolstoy, and Kafka. His Job sits in a bleak landscape, accompanied by his friends. Beside the comforters there is a basket of scrolls. The angel of death looms in the background, while the eye of God appears from out of the clouds.[80]

Yehua Epstein provided an equally stark evocation of the post-Holocaust despairing Job, as did Benno Elkan in a Menorah presented to the Israeli Knesset in Jerusalem in 1956. Nathan Rappaort's *Job*, a sculpted piece, is one of the most striking late 20th-century Jewish representations of the man from Uz. Rappaport's Job presses his fists against his chest and looks to the heavens for help that does not come. Magda Litz, a contemporary French sculptor, produced an evocative *Job, the Innocent Sufferer,* in the 1960s. The lone figure's arms are twisted at grotesque angles, and Job's mouth is open in mid-scream.[81]

Abraham Rattner produced a series of abstract Jobs throughout the mid-twentieth century. His *Job #9* is the most evocative of these. The patriarch appears with his wife, who has two separate faces, one sympathetic, the other accusatory. Job's face is without expression. He seems lost in an inner turmoil that cannot be touched by his wife, or anyone else.[82]

Perhaps the ultimate post-Holocaust Job is to be found in Misch Kohn's woodcut print of the man from Uz (cat. 44). Job stands with his arms encircling his upper torso, head fallen to his chest, the figure is bent slightly at the waist, his body creating the effect of a nuclear mushroom cloud, the ultimate symbol, and reality, of innocent suffering.[83]

Ben Shahn takes up this same theme in his 1964 painting *Where Wast Thou?* (cat. 46).[84] The Hebrew at the bottom of the painting quotes God's speech in chapter 38 of the Book of Job: "Where were you when I laid the foundations of the earth…?"

In the ancient Hebrew book, God questions Job, but over two millennia later, in this evocative rendering of the voice from the whirlwind, Shahn turns the tables. Only the thumb of God is visible in the midst of the maelstrom from which he speaks. The only hint of the divine presence amidst the chaos at the center of the work, God's thumb is so lightly pressed that it may not leave prints. In this stunningly beautiful painting, completed 20 years after Hiroshima and Nagasaki, in the midst of the Cold War, Shahn asks of the divine: Where were you?

Notes

1. Nathan Rappaport, *Job*, (twentieth century) Yad Vashem, Jerusalem.
2. For more general remarks on the Naphtali and Asher versions of the Book of Job, see S. Baer's notes to his *Liber Iob* (Leipzig: Tauchnitz, 1875). Baer gives the fullest accounting of the differences between the two different schools of Masoretes on Job.
3. The Revised Standard translation.
4. RSV translation.
5. The edition of the Septuagint used in this essay is that of Alfred Rahlfs (Stuttgart: Deutsche Bibelgesellschaft, 1935).
6. The edition of the Vulgate used in this essay is the 1881 Roman edition based on the definitive text produced in 1604, during the papacy of Clement VIII.
7. Luther's preface to the Old Testament (1523), revised by him in 1545. *Luther's Works*, volume 35, edited by E.T. Bachmann (Philadelphia: Muhlenberg Press, 1960), pp. 235-251.
8. Ibid.
9. Ibid.
10. Ibid.
11. *Luther's Works*, volume 54, edited and translated by T.G. Tappert (Philadephia: Fortress Press, 1967), pp. 128-129.
12. The translation of the *Testament* used here is that of R.A. Kraft, Society of Biblical Literature, Texts and Translation Series, #4 (Missoula, Montana, 1974).
13. Revised Standard Version translation.
14. Baba Bathra 15b.
15. Ibid.
16. Ibid.
17. Peskita Rabba 190a.
18. Baba Bathra 15b, 16a.
19. Ibid.
20. The translation of the Moralia used in this essay is that of Charles Marriott (Oxford: J.H. Parker Publishers, 1848).
21. Ibid, introduction, p. ii.
22. Nahum Glatzer, *The Dimensions of Job* (New York: Schocken Books, 1968), pp. 31-32.
23. The edition of the Qu'ran used in this essay is *The Holy Qu'ran-Text, Translation, and Commentary* edited and translated by Addullah Yusaf Ali (Cambridge: Murray Printing House, 1947).
24. Ibid. p. 173.
25. Ibid. p. 191.
26. Ibid. p. 209.
27. Ibid. p. 223-224.
28. For these early images, see Samuel Terrien's *The Iconography of Job Through the Centuries* (University Park: Penn State University Press, 1996).
29. *Job Seated*, fresco (third century) Cemetery of Domitilla, Rome.
30. *Job, His Wife, The Tempter, and Adam and Eve*, bas relief (fourth century) Sarcophagus of Junius Bassus, Saint Peter's Sacristy, the Vatican.
31. See pp. 35-56 of Terrien.
32. *Anti-Christ Seated Above Leviathan,* and *Devil Riding Behemoth, Liber Floridus,* (twelfth century) Ghent University Library; *Anti-Christ Riding Leviathan,* (twelfth century) Bodleian Library; *Leviathan As The Jaws of Hell,* (twelfth century) pulpit slab, Cathedral at Traetto-Minturo.
33. *Job and His Wife,* (fourteenth century) Staatsbibiotek Preussischer Kulturbesitz.
34. Job 39: 13-18.
35. *Job, His Wife, and Satan,* (fifteenth century) *Le Miroir de l'humaine salvation,* Musée Condé, Chantilly, France.
36. *Job and His Friends,* (ca. 1300) The Walters Art Museum; Sauvigny Bible, (twelfth century), Chantilly, Musée Condé, frontispiece for Book of Job.
37. Ibid., text of Book of Job; Bartolo di Fredi, *Job and His Friends*, Basilica Collegiata di S. Maria Assunta, Tuscany.
38. Book of Hours (1400), Library of Congress. See also Gregory the Great's comments on 19:25-26 for this castle metaphor.
39. Jean Fouquet, *Job on the Heap of Refuse and His Three Comforters, The Hours of Etienne Chevalier,* Chantilly, Musée Condé; book of hours (1524), Library of Congress, Rosenwald Collection.
40. Jean Colombe, *Job on His Dungheap, Book of Hours of Henry VII,* Bibliothéque Nationale, Paris.
41. Jean Bourdichon, *Job on His Dunghill*, book of hours, Bibliothéque Nationale, Paris.
42. *Saint Job and Two Petitioners*, German woodcut (1490), reproduced in Aesculape, volume 20 (1930), p. 48.
43. Pierre de Nesson, *Neuf Leçons de Job*, (fifteenth century) Bibliothèque Nationale, Paris; Albrecht Dürer, *Two Musicians Comfort Job*, altarpiece (1510) Wallraf-Richartz Museum, Cologne.
44. Anton Koberger, Nuremberg Bible, (1483) Library of Congress, Lessing J. Rosenwald Collection, Rare Book and Special Collections Division.

45. *The Restored Job*, (fifteenth century) Rothschild Manuscript, National Museum of Israel.
46. al-Nishapuri, *Qisas al-Anbiya* (The Legends of the Prophets), (1580) New York Public Library, Spencer Collection.
47. *Ayyub*, (sixteenth century) Chester Beatty Library, Dublin.
48. Hans Wechbelin, *Job and His Woes*, (ca. 1550) German National Museum, Nuremberg.
49. *Job* (woodcut, 1537), Kupferstichkalinett Staatliche Museen Preussischer Kulturbesitz, Berlin.
50. Hans Holbein (ii), *Icones historarium* (1543), Walters Art Museum, Baltimore.
51. Augustin Hirschvogel, *Job Learns of His Misfortunes*, (1549), National Gallery of Art, Washington, D.C. Lessing J. Rosenwald Collection, Washington, D.C.
52. Hans Sebald Beham, *Job Conversing with His Friends*, (1547), Philadelphia Museum of Art.
53. Maerten van Heemskerck, *The Triumph of Job*, (1559) National Gallery of Art, Washington, D.C.
54. Lucas Vorsterman, *Job Tormented By Demons and Abused By His Wife*, (1620) Philadelphia Museum of Art.
55. Fra Bartolommeo, *Job, The Prophet*, (date unknown) Vatican Museum; Girolamo Libri, *S. Sebastian, S.Roch, and S. Job*, (1505) Church of S. Tomasso Canturicense, Verona; Giovanni Bellini, *Pala di S. Giobbe*, (1497) Academia, Venice.
56. Vittore Carpaccio, *Job and the Dead Christ*, (1505-10) Staatliche Museen, Berlin.
57. Peter Paul Rubens, *Job and Musicians*, (date unknown) Wallraf-Richartz Museum, Cologne; Bernard van Orley, *Job, His Wife, and Musicians*, altarpiece, (date unknown) Musées Royaux des Beaux-Arts, Brussels; Jan Mandyn, *Job, His Wife, and Musicians*, (1470-1500) Musée de la Chartreuse, Douai.
58. Luis Giordano, *Job and His Comforters*, (1680) the Sacristy of the Monastery at San Lorenzo, Escorial.
59. See note 54.
60. Guido Reni, *The Triumph of Job*, (date unknown) Nôtre Dame, Paris; Guiseppe Maria Mitelli, *The Triumph of Job*, (c.1679) Philadelphia Museum of Art.
61. Georges de La Tour, *Job and His Wife*, (1635) Musée departmental des Vosges, Epinal. Jacques Thuillier and Pierre Rosenberg, eds. *Catalogue Georges de La Tour* (Paris: Editions des Musées Nationaux, 1972), pp. 211-212.
62. Gaspare Travesi, *Job and His Wife*, (date unknown) The Vatican Library.
63. See pp. 161 to 176 of Terrien.
64. Ibid; Ibid.
65. Gerard René Le Vilain, *Iob*, (date unknown) Baltimore Museum of Art.
66. *A Curious Hieroglyphic Bible...* (London: Bassam and Hymonds, 1796) Library of Congress.
67. William Blake, *Job* (1825) National Gallery of Art, Washington, D.C.
68. Joseph Wicksteed, *Blake's Vision of the Book of Job* (London: J.M. Dent, 1910.)
69. Both Donne and Milton had sustained interest in the Book of Job. Donne's extant Sermons contain more than 200 references to the man from Uz. Milton, throughout *Paradise Regained* and *Samson Agonistes*, identifies Job with both Samson and Jesus.
70. See pp. 39-45 of Glatzer.
71. Christian Ernest Stölzel, *Job* (1833), Philadelphia Museum of Art.
72. Paul Falconer Poole, *Job and His Friends*, (date unknown), The Library of the Jewish Theological Seminary of America, New York.
73. James Tissot, *Job and His Family*, (date unknown), The Jewish Museum, New York.
74. Alexandre Gabriel Decamps, *Job, His Wife, and Friends*, (1885), Minneapolis Institute of Arts.
75. Franz Gruber, *Job: My Lament is a Success*, (1944), The Tate Gallery, London.
76. Alphonse Legros, *Job, First Plate*, (date unknown) National Gallery of Art, Washington, D.C.
77. François Nermeylen, *Job Dejected*, (1880) Museum voor Kerkelyske Kunst, Leuven.
78. Oskar Koloschka, *Woman and Man*, (1909) owned by Mrs. Kokoschka, Zurich.
79. Ivan Mestrovic, *Job*, (1945) Syracuse University Art Collection.
80. Fritz Eichenberg, *The Book of Job*, (1955) National Gallery of Art, Washington, D.C.
81. See note 1.
82. Abraham Rattner, *Job #9*, (1959) Kennedy Galleries, New York.
83. Misch Kohn, *Job*, (1959), Library of Congress, Prints and Photographs Division.
84. Ben Shahn, *Where Wast Thou?* (1964) Amon Carter Museum, Fort Worth, Texas.

Selected Bibliography

The Babylonian Talmud edited by I. Epstein (London: Soncino Press, 1936.)

Besserman, Lawrence. *The Legend of Job in the Middle Ages* (Cambridge: Harvard University Press, 1979.)

Dhorme, Paul. *Le Livre de Job* (Paris: Victor Lecoffre, 1926.)

Fine, H.A. "The Tradition of a Patient Job," *Journal of Biblical Literature* 74 (1955.)

Ginsberg, H.L. "Job the Patient and Job the Impatient," *Conservative Judaism* 21 (1967.)

Glatzer, Nahum. *The Dimensions of Job* (New York: Schocken Books, 1969.)

Gordis, Robert. *The Book of God and Man: A Study of Job* (Chicago: University of Chicago Press, 1965.)

_____ . *The Book of Job: Commentary, New Translation, and Special Studies* (New York: Jewish Theological Seminary, 1978.)

Gregory the Great. *Morals on the Book of Job.* Edited and translated by Charles Marriott (Oxford: J.H. Parker, 1848.)

Habel, Norman. *The Book of Job* (Cambridge: Cambridge University Press, 1975.)

Hanson, Anthony. *The Book of Job: Introduction and Commentary.* London: SCM Press, 1953.)

Leclercq, Henri. "Job" in *Dictionnaire d'archeologie chretienne et de liturgie*. Edited by Fernand Cabrol et al. 15 volumes (Paris: Letoyuzey et Ane, 1903-1953.)

Levenson, Jon Douglas. *The Book of Job in its Time and in the Twentieth Century* (Cambridge: Harvard University Press, 1972.)

MacDonald, D.B. "Some External Evidence on the Original Form of the Legend of Job," *American Journal of Semitic Languages and Literature* 14 (1898.)

Meyer, Kathi. "Saint Job as a Patron of Music," *The Art Bulletin* 36 (1954.)

The Koran. Translated by Arthur Arberry (London: Oxford University press, 1964.)

Maimonides, Moses. *The Guide for the Perplexed* translated by M. Friedlander (New York: Dover Books, 1956.)

Poesch, Jessie. "The Beasts From Job in the Liber Floridus Manuscripts," *Journal of the Warburg and Courtauld Institutes* (33) 1970.

Pope, Marvin. *Job: Introduction, Translation and Notes* (Garden City: Doubleday, 1973.)

Reau, Louis. "Job" in *Iconographie de l'art chretien* (Paris: Presses universitaires, 1956.)

Rowley, H.H. *Job* (London" Thomas Nelson, 1970.)

Sanders, Paul S., editor *Twentieth Century Interpretations of the Book of Job* (Englewood Cliffs: Prentice Hall, 1968.)

Snaith, Norman Henry. *The Book of Job: Its Origin and Purpose* (London: SCM Press, 1968.)

Stevenson, William Barron. *Critical Notes on the Hebrew Texts of the Poem of Job* (Aberdeen: Aberdeen University press, 1951.)

Terrien, Samuel. "Introduction and Exegesis of the Book of Job," *The Interpreter's Bible* (New York: Abingdon Press, 1954.)

_____ . *The Iconography of Job Through the Centuries* (University Park: Pennsylvania State University Press, 1996.)

The Testament of Job. Translated and edited by R.A. Kraft (Missoula: Society of Biblical Literature, 1974.)

Tur-Sinai, Naphtali Herz. *The Book of Job: A New Commentary* (Jerusalem: Kirtath Sepher, 1967.)

Vicchio, Stephen. *The Voice From the Whirlwind* (Westminster: Christian Classics, 1989.)

Wright, Andrew. *Blake's Job: A Commentary* (Oxford: Clarendon Press, 1972.)

Zuckerman, Bruce. *Job the Silent: A Study in Historical Counterpoint* (Oxford: Oxford University Press, 1991.)

1.

Job and His Three Friends

1300, Monastic Psalter,
Purchased S. & A.P. Fund
The Walters Art Museum
Baltimore, Maryland

Psalters were the primary books used for private prayer and devotion prior to the emergence of the book of hours in the thirteenth century. In addition to including the psalms, for which they are named, psalters often contained other texts such as calendars and litanies. The Byzantine psalters are most noted for their iconography of biblical scenes and natural rendering of figures. Due to an error in early Greek translations of the Job text, the comforters are displayed as kings rather than comforters.

The Byzantine Empire, where Constantine the Great founded Constantinople in 330 C.E., fused Greek, Roman, and Christian elements. Though its language was Greek, as the eastern capital of the Roman Empire, this culture influenced a wide region including Asia Minor and Italy.

Byzantine images are rare because many political and religious leaders during the Iconoclastic Controversy in the eighth and ninth centuries opposed the use of religious images, and the schism between the eastern and western churches prevented the Byzantine culture from spreading to the west. Later, under the Palaeologan Dynasty in the late Middle Ages, culture and monasticism flourished. Ultimately, Constantinople was seized by the Ottoman Turks in 1453, resulting in the fall of the Byzantine Empire.

Job and His Friends
(in initial V)

c. 1300, Bible, Northern Italy
Bequest of Henry Walters
The Walters Art Museum,
Baltimore, Maryland
W.151, f.239

By 600 C.E., Latin was the only language used for the western Christian liturgy. Most interpretations of Job from the end of the sixth century until the late fourteenth century were based on the exegetical work of Gregory the Great. His allegorical commentary was as widely read as the biblical text itself. This folio from a northern Italian Bible features an historiated initial "V" with illuminated details depicting Job and his comforters. The grotesque, here shown holding the tapestry with its teeth, was a popular element in Gothic art. Job is shown with sores and halo, in a prefiguration of Christ.

Book of Hours

1400, French, Rare Book and Special Collections Division, Library of Congress, Washington, D.C.

This page includes an initial decorated letter, zoomorphic figures, and a foliated border depicting Job's comforters in rabbi's caps pointing at him in blame. Job has no sores and is seated on a bed of wheat rather than a dungheap, symbolic of the separation of the wheat and chaff at the end of time.

The border includes strawberries and violets, the symbols of humility. The bird in early Christian art often symbolized the winged soul and suggested the importance of a spiritual rather than material focus. Many verses from the Book of Job are included in the Office of the Dead, but this portion is particularly emphasized: "For I know my Redeemer lives, and at the last he will stand upon the earth; and after my skin has been destroyed, then, in my flesh, I shall see God." (Job 19:25-27).

This Latin book of hours, also known as a primer or *horae*, was modeled after the devotions from the eight canonical hours of the Divine Office. The central theme focused on the Little Office of the Blessed Virgin Mary and was used by lay persons who wished to emulate the religious practices of the clergy. As the popularity of this devotion grew, other elements, including a calendar, Litany of the Saints, Psalms, and The Office of the Dead were added.

Bible, German

1483, Anton Koberger (1445-1513), Nuremberg
Lessing J. Rosenwald Collection, Rare Book and Special Collections Division
Library of Congress, Washington, D.C.

This large panoramic image was hand-colored and includes a sympathetic wife. Job is sitting on a heap of wheat against a backdrop of burning houses, and he has no sores. The knight, bishop, and pilgrim symbolize the journey of the soul, while the dove with the olive branch represents purity and peace.

In 1470 Anton Koberger established the first print shop in Nuremberg and in 1483 he published a German Bible with woodcut illustrations. Koberger gained a high social standing due to the success of his business, a shop reputed to have 24 presses where more than 100 printers worked.

5.

Book of Hours

1524, French
Lessing J. Rosenwald
Collection, Rare Book &
Special Collections Division
Library of Congress,
Washington, D.C.

The Christ-like Job is covered with sores and robed in white. He is pictured with sympathizing comforters and wife. As with many sixteenth and seventeenth century European images of Job, a castle is included in the background to inspire a vision of eternal reward.

 The Latin book of hours, which enjoyed popularity among devout and wealthy French laymen, remained relatively unchanged from the time of its conception in the thirteenth century until the sixteenth century. The illustration is framed with gold leaf columns, a typical element in books of hours. The seashell seen on the facing page generally signifies a pilgrimage, in this case, that of the soul.

Satan plagt Job aus verhengnus Gottes. Job 1.

Satan plagues Job with God's permission. Job 1. (Synopsis of Job 1, in German)

Biblisch Historien, figürlich fürgebiblet

1533, Beham, Hans Sebald (1500-1550)
Engraving
Lessing J. Rosenwald Collection, Rare Book of Special Collections Division Library of Congress, Washington, D.C.

This small volume of woodcut German Bible illustrations portrays a clear-skinned Job covered with a loincloth, sitting on a layer of wheat under a humble shelter. The wheat is the reminder of the separation of saved and damned at the Judgement Day.

Together with his younger brother Barthel Beham and George Pencz, Hans Behan was known as one of the "Little Masters" because of the diminutive size of his engravings and etchings. The artists shared radical views on religion and government with reformist theologians Andreas Karlstadt and Thomas Müntzer, both followers of Martin Luther; Müntzer was also a leader in peasant uprisings. These "godless painters," as they were called, were banned from Nuremberg because critics maintained that they did not believe in baptism, Christ, or transubstantion. Beham nevertheless continued to create religious illustrations, including an edition of Luther's Bible in 1527.

7.

Icones historarium

C.1543
Hans Holbein (ii) (1497/8-1543), Lyons
Bequest of Henry Walters
The Walters Art Museum, Baltimore, Maryland
(92.24.1)

Satan does away with all Job's goods and strikes his children,
having received permission from the Lord.
He praises God in his affliction.
(Synopsis of Job 1, in Latin)

By Satan (having received permission from God)
Suffers great persecution in his goods:
Loses his children, about which he is patient,
Praising his God in this affliction.
(Synopsis of Job 1 and 2, in French)

In this illustration appearing in a history of sacred images, several scenes are represented as occurring simultaneously. Job is seen sitting on a dungheap, suffering the pain of his sores and the ridicule of his wife and friends. In the background, the destruction of the houses and stables is shown.

Hans Holbein the Younger, known for his paintings and portraits for the English court, produced the *Icones*, a series of images based on the Hebrew Bible. This narrative is modeled after a Bible designed by Nuremberg artists Erhard Schön and Hans Springinklee, and published by Anton Koberger in 1518 and 1520.

Sketches for the *Icones* date between 1526-1530 and incorporate the Reformation attitude that Job could not be completely blameless because he suffered the stain of original sin. This image of Job is the first of three included in the *Icones* and was probably engraved by Hans Lützelburger in Basle, Switzerland.

Job Conversing with His Friends

1547

Hans Sebald Beham (1500-1550), Engraving

Philadelphia Museum of Art: The Muriel and Philip Berman Gift, acquired from the John S. Phillips bequest of 1876 to the Pennsylvania Academy of the Fine Arts, with funds contributed by Muriel and Philip Berman, gifts (by exchange) of Lisa Norris Elkins, Bryant W. Langston, Samuel S. White 3rd and Vera White, with additional funds contributed by John Howard McFadden, Jr., Thomas Skelton Harrison, and the Philip H. and A.S.W. Rosenbach Foundation, 1985. 1985-052-33453

Philadelphia, Pennsylvania

For you have not spoken rightly in public, as has my servant Job.
(Synopsis of Job 42, in Latin)

This vignette by Beham depicts Job on a pillow conversing with friends, in contrast with an earlier image where Job is alone. Job's wife is shown in the background with her arms stretched out as if distressed at the plight of her husband. The ring of keys at her waist are a symbol of her authority. Typical of medieval illuminated manuscripts is the partially destroyed castle, a symbol of the loss of Job's children and destruction of his property. God appears faintly in the background with breath coming from his mouth, suggesting the voice from the whirlwind.

Hans Sebald Beham was a printmaker, miniaturist, and designer of glass paintings in Nuremberg, Germany. Recognized as one of the most productive printmakers of his generation, Beham created over 270 engravings and etchings and 1000 woodcuts.

> Prouer. 3.b. Das gůt haß ich empfangen von Gott
> Iob. 1. 2. c. Drumß ich jm danckßar sol sein in not
> Bloß bin ich auß můter leyß komen
> Nichts haß ich mit mir wegk genommen.

9.

Job Learns of His Misfortunes

1549
Augustin Hirschvogel
(1503-1533)
Etching
Rosenwald Collection 1950
National Gallery of Art, Washington
1950.17.194

Everything good I have received from God
That is why I should be thankful to him even
in times of need.
(Synopsis of Proverbs 3, in German)

I have just sprung from my mother's womb,
Taking nothing with me.
(Synopsis of Job 3:11 and 10:18, in German)

This allegorical image depicts a patient Job with his wife and the messengers delivering the news of his misfortunes. The text included with the image states only that God is responsible for good, and omits the portion of the text in which Job says to his wife, "Shall we receive good at the hand of God, and shall we not receive evil?" (Job 2:10). Behind Job's wife is one messenger with a rabbi's cap and another carrying a dead child.

A member of the Danube school, Hirschvogel was a majolica painter who later established himself as a cartographer, for which he became renowned.

10.

Qisas al Anbyia (The Legends of the Prophets)

1580
al-Nishapuri
Persian MS 46 f. 109
Spencer Collection,
The New York Public Library,
Astor, Lenox and Tilden
Foundations
New York City, New York

In Moslem art, Job is usually shown standing in a spring that flows around the patriarch's feet, following the Qu'ran's suggestion that he was healed by holy waters. The Arabic text is accompanied by a flowering tree, symbolizing restoration and hope for new life, and is often an important element in these Islamic depictions.

Extant Islamic representations of Job (Ayyub) from the twelfth to the sixteenth century tend toward the depiction of the patriarch's restored state. Moslem understandings of Job were derived, for the most part, from his treatment in the Qu'ran, where Job is described as a holy man of extraordinary patience. In Islamic manuscripts, the patriarch is most often depicted accompanied by the angel Jibrail (Gabriel), and attended by his faithful wife, Rahman.

The Triumph of Job

1559
Maerten van Heemskerck
(1498-1574)
Pen and brown ink with traces of chalk on laid paper
National Gallery of Art, Washington
Gift of Walter H. and Leonore Annenberg in Honor of the 50th Anniversary of the National Gallery of Art 1990
1990.47.3

Heemskerck's composition continues the association of Job as a Christ figure and the wife and comforters as allies of Satan, with the wife extending her hands in disparagement and the comforters wearing rabbi's caps. In images from this period, banners are generally carried to show triumph, and the scales suggest Job's questions to God about justice. The backdrop of destruction illustrates the opening chapters from the story of Job. Heemskerck's use of the allegorical tortoise—"slow and steady wins the race"—is a visual testimony to Job's patience.

Heemskerck, a painter from the Netherlands, devoted much of his career to religious and allegorical themes and was inspired by the poet and humanist Dirck Volckertz Coornhert. Over 600 of Heemskerck's drawings were transferred to copper plates in order to make prints. Heemskerck, like Peter Bruegel and Hans Sebald Beham, was a witness to the upheaval during the Reformation and Counter Reformation under the rule of Charles V and his son Phillip II.

Omnibus amiſsis, poſt mille pericula, rebus:
Poſt tot difficiles caſus, varios cruciatus,
IOB quibus infeſto tentatus Dæmone, Amicis,

Coniuge fallaci, paſſus tamen eſt fide cuncta
Conſtanter, firmusq́; nimis teſtudinis inſtar,
Manſit, quam poterit tectam cōfringere nemo.

12.

Triumph of Job
1559
Dirck Volckertz Coornhert (1522-1590), after Maerten van Heemskerck (1498-1574)
Engraving
National Gallery of Art, Washington
Ailsa Mellon Bruce Fund 1974

Having lost all things, after a thousand trials: after so many severe misfortunes, various torments, Job, tempted by the hostile demon, by his friends, by his deceitful wife,

Nevertheless suffered all things firmly in faith and steadfastly, much after the manner of the tortoise whose shell none can destroy, he endured.
(Subscript: Latin)

This plate faithfully follows the original drawing created by Maerten van Heemskerck. This print is part of an eight-page series called *The Triumph of Patience*, which includes the triumphs of Isaac, Joseph, David, Tobit, St. Stephen, and Jesus Christ. Heemskerck produced many images of Job including a print in his series, the *Eight Beatitudes* and another series dedicated exclusively to the Book of Job.

Coornhert, a poet, humanist, and active supporter of religious tolerance, was an accomplished engraver and book illustrator. He provided inspiration to artists whose designs exemplified his own ethical and religious ideas. Although there were different engravers and printers for each plate in these series, Coornhert worked as the principal engraver for Heemskerck, and is among the most famous.

13.

Job Tormented by Demons and Abused by His Wife

c.1620, Lucas Vorsterman (I) (1595-1675), Engraving

Philadelphia Museum of Art: The Muriel and Philip Berman Gift, acquired from the John S. Phillips bequest of 1876 to the Pennsylvania Academy of the Fine Arts, with funds contributed by Muriel and Philip Berman, gifts (by exchange) of Lisa Norris Elkins, Bryant W. Langston, Samuel S. White 3rd and Vera White, with additional funds contributed by John Howard McFadden, Jr., Thomas Skelton Harrison, and the Philip H. and A.S.W. Rosenbach Foundation, 1985. 1985-052-09972

Philadelphia, Pennsylvania

Man born of a woman is short-lived and full of trouble. Like a flower that springs up and fades, swift as a shadow that does not abide.
(Job 14:1, in Latin)

The powerful diagonal position of Job reflects the emotional tenor of the Counter Reformation, and adds a dramatic realism to the scene. This engraving, whose composition is neither conventional nor static, reflects Rubens' devout Roman Catholic sympathy. Here Job, clothed in a white loincloth, is spurned by his wife and the demons, in a prefigurative flagellation of Christ. The work's philosophical and visual elements are consistent with other images of this period; mound of wheat, destroyed columns, and the wife's posture as she gestures in exasperation and accusation.

This engraving by Lucas Vosterman is taken after a triptych by Peter Paul Rubens. The painting, which was destroyed in the bombardment of 1695 by Louis XIV, was originally commissioned by the Brussels Musician's Guild, who claimed Job as their patron saint. Vorsterman was probably Rubens' greatest and most prolific engraver. After a conflict over the ownership of printed works, their collaboration ended and Rubens was forced to obtain protection from the courts after the engraver made threats to his life.

Triumph of Job

c. 1679

Giuseppe Maria Mitelli (1634-1718) after Guido Reni (1575-1642), Etching

Philadelphia Museum of Art: The Muriel and Philip Berman Gift, acquired from the John S. Phillips bequest of 1876 to the Pennsylvania Academy of the Fine Arts, with funds contributed by Muriel and Philip Berman, gifts (by exchange) of Lisa Norris Elkins, Bryant W. Langston, Samuel S. White 3rd and Vera White, with additional funds contributed by John Howard McFadden, Jr., Thomas Skelton Harrison, and the Philip H. and A.S.W. Rosenbach Foundation, 1985
1985-052-32658

Philadelphia, Pennsylvania

This triumphant hallowed Job is more a king or Christ figure than a suffering man. Job was "sainted" in many works throughout this period, although he was never officially canonized. A grand feast offered by servants and family is set in a structure of restored arches supported by Corinthian columns. The sheep and cow in the foreground are a reference to the line, "offer up a sacrifice for yourselves and let my servant Job pray for you" (Job 42:9).

Reni, the artist of the original painting, is known for his sensual style and compositional grace. He was an extremely religious Italian painter and engraver who studied briefly under Carracci, and in his later years became a rival of Caravaggio. This engraving, produced by Mitelli, was completed a few years after Reni's death.

Mitelli, an Italian Renaissance print-maker and sculptor from Bologna, studied under his father Agostino Stanzani and several other prominent artists of the day. He left a large print oeuvre that illustrated religious ceremonies, folkloric tales, and biblical scenes.

15.

Job on the Dung Hill, Surrounded by His Friends and Wife

17th century (?)

Anonymous, after Peter Paul Rubens,

Engraving

Philadelphia Museum of Art:
The Muriel and Philip Berman Gift, acquired from the John S. Phillips bequest of 1876 to the Pennsylvania Academy of the Fine Arts, with funds contributed by Muriel and Philip Berman, gifts (by exchange) of Lisa Norris Elkins, Bryant W. Langston, Samuel S. White 3rd and Vera White, with additional funds contributed by John Howard McFadden, Jr., Thomas Skelton Harrison, and the Philip H. and A.S.W. Rosenbach Foundation, 1985.

1985-052-42499

Philadelphia, Pennsylvania

There is no need of a tile to scrape Job's wounds,
The querulous tongue of his nagging wife chafes its border.

Why do you stand around friends, tempting me?
Or is it because the fly who flees my sores is gone?
(Synopses of Job 2 and 5, in Latin)

This Christ-like Job sitting on a stack of hay with outstretched arms is chastised by his wife. "Why are you still hanging on to your integrity? Why don't you curse God and die?" (Job 2:9). Castle ruins and broken pottery shards, the symbols of destruction, are once again included, as the comforters look on critically.

"Job" after Fra Bartolommeo

Date unknown
Gerard René Le Vilain, French (1740-1836)
Engraving
Baltimore Museum of Art:
Garrett Collection
BMA 1946.112.3155
Baltimore, Maryland

Job is a patriarchal figure in this work. His banner proclaiming "Ipse Erit Salvator Meus" (He will be my savior) is a testimony to Job's faith in spite of his trials, and a harbinger of his resurrection.

This engraving was reproduced by the French engraver Gerard René Le Vilain after the painting *The Prophet Job* by Fra Bartolommeo, the late sixteenth-century Italian Dominican monk and artist.

17.

A Curious Hieroglyphic Bible,

or, Select Passages in the Old and New Testaments, represented with emblematical figures, for the amusement of youth: designed chiefly to familiarize tender age, in a pleasing and diverting manner, with early ideas of the Holy Scriptures: to which are subjoined, a short account of the lives of the Evangelists, and other pieces, illustrated with cuts.

13th edition, 1804

Published: London: Printed and sold by Robert Bassam ... H.D. Symonds ... Scatcherd and Whitaker .. and may be had of all the booksellers, 1796

Rare Book & Special Collections Division

Library of Congress, Washington, D.C.
RBSC BS 560 1804. Page 50

This printed book from the late eighteenth century was intended to be an entertaining biblical tutorial for children. Each page is dedicated to a different story from the Bible. The English subtext is in the form of a rebus: "I put on righteousness and it clothed me: My judgement was as a robe and a diadem. I was eyes to the blind and feet was I to the lame." (Job 29:14-15).

Until the late eighteenth century, printing technology had not changed much since Gutenberg's printing press. Under Queen Elizabeth I, the daughter of King Henry VIII, the Geneva Bible was distributed. Queen Elizabeth I was succeeded by King James I, who sought to produce a Bible that enjoyed the same popularity, and he authorized a translation intended to end all translations with the use of all available interpretations and private research. The authorized version, which became known as the King James Version, was printed in 1611. The widespread use of this translation was slow at first, but eventually the King James Version became the English Bible for standard use, which it remained for over 250 years until the publication of the Revised Standard Version in 1881.

The romantic writer, artist, and mystic William Blake dedicated the latter years of his life to illustrating the Book of Job, beginning with a set of watercolors for John Linnell. A landscape painter and engraver, Linnell was 25 years old and Blake 61 when their alliance began on the Job illustrations. This unique partnership became a life-changing event for Blake, making him both productive and prosperous. Blake's illustrations for the Book of Job are considered the magnum opus of his artwork. Blake died two years after its completion.

Blake's early interest in Job was expressed as a collection of sometimes tangled reflections on the Book of Job, his romantic ideal of suffering, interpretations of the writings of John Milton, and his glosses on the theories of Norwegian spiritualist Emanuel Swedenborg. Blake incorporated his own commentary and symbolic imagery into the biblical text. His *Book of Job* is comprised of 21 plates and divided into three categories, with seven illustrations each: Chaos (plates 1-7), Lucidity (plates 8-14), and Resolution (plates 15-21).

18.

Satan Before the Throne of God

1825
William Blake (1757-1827)
Engraving on India Paper
National Gallery of Art,
Washington
Gift of W.G. Russell Allen,
1941
(1941. 1. 227)

This complex image illustrates the opening scene of the wager between Satan and God over the unsuspecting Job below: "There was a day when the Sons of God came to present themselves before the Lord and Satan came also among them to present himself before the Lord" (Job 1:6). Unlike most previous artists, Blake treated Job's wife with sensitivity and compassion, and in this image he has positioned her beside Job as a model of fidelity and sympathy. There is a striking similarity between the faces of Job and God. Above Job appear the accuser Satan and God, who is holding a book of divine order in his lap. The margin illustration represents the pastoral life of Job and his wife. In traditional Christian symbolism, the peacock represents vanity and foolish pride.

Satan Smiting Job with Boils

1825
William Blake (1757-1827)
Engraving on India Paper
National Gallery of Art, Washington
Gift of W.G. Russell Allen, 1941
(1941.1. 231)

In addition to the obvious story illustrations are the allegories hidden in the creatures, plants, and architectural elements Blake has chosen to include within the story or in the margins. Some of these elements, like the sepulcher in the background, appear frequently throughout Blake's book. The bats in the marginal illustrations are associated with the night of spiritual darkness, while the spider alludes to one of Blake's theories about creation, with a woman weaving the threads of the material body. The locusts refer to the plagues upon the Egyptians, while the fish symbolizes both Christ and the Leviathan.

The Lord Answering Job Out of the Whirlwind

1825
William Blake (1757-1827)
Engraving on India Paper
National Gallery of Art, Washington
Gift of W.G. Russell Allen, 1941
(1941.1.238)

Who maketh the Clouds and Chariot & walketh on the Wings of the Wind
(Psalm 104:3)

Blake has incorporated the tree, a Christian symbol used in early texts, at the base of the illustration. The tree has long served as a representation of life or death, depending upon whether or not the tree is healthy. Blake consistently depicts Job's wife as a constant and loving companion.

The biblical passage about God speaking as a voice from the whirlwind has been used by many artists as a subject for Job illustrations: "Then the Lord answered Job out of the whirlwind...Where were you?" (Job 38:1-4).

Job's Sacrifice

1825
William Blake (1757-1827)
Engraving on India Paper
National Gallery of Art, Washington
Gift of W.G. Russell Allen, 1941
(1941.1.243)

This illustration from Blake's epilogue represents God rebuking Job's friends, who have not spoken rightly of the patriarch and his plight. The comforters are ordered to offer sacrifice while Job prays for them (Job 42:7). The loyal, unwavering wife is cast in light, while the accusing comforters are cast in darkness. The prefiguration of Christ is exemplified in Job's outstretched arms. The sacrificial flame, with its triangular shape, can be interpreted as representing light and spirit.

Job and His Daughters

1825
William Blake (1757-1827)
Engraving on India Paper
National Gallery of Art,
Washington
Gift of W.G. Russell Allen,
1941
(1941.1.245)

Praise him with lyre and harp
(Psalm 150:3)

This illustration, also from Blake's epilogue, shows Job's three beautiful daughters listening to his tale. The background panels tell of disasters; the central panel includes God and the voice from the whirlwind. The grapevine, in early Christian tradition, symbolizes Christ. The lyre and harp in the bottom corner have several biblical references in addition to the one that appears in the engraving: "They sing to the tambourine and the lyre" (Job 21:12), and "my lyre has turned to mourning, and my pipe to the voice of those who weep" (Job 30:31).

According to the Book of Job, the daughters Jemimah, Keziah, and Kerenhappech all receive an inheritance like their brothers, an atypical practice among Jews of the ancient period.

Job and His Wife Restored to Posterity

1825
William Blake (1757-1827)
Engraving on India Paper
National Gallery of Art, Washington
Gift of W.G. Russell Allen, 1941
(1941.1.246)

This scene of Job restored and "blessed two-fold" includes his daughters, sons, and wife. Job has his left arm raised in glory of God, while his right arm strums the harp in praise. Job's wife, strategically placed on his right side, shows her allegiance. The ram and bull, signs of strength, are offered in sacrifice.

Job

1833

Christian Ernst Stölzel (1792-1837) after Gustav Marie Jäger (1808-1871)

Etching and Engraving

Philadelphia Museum of Art: The Muriel and Philip Berman Gift, acquired from the John S. Phillips bequest of 1876 to the Pennsylvania Academy of the Fine Arts, with funds contributed by Muriel and Philip Berman, gifts (by exchange) of Lisa Norris Elkins, Bryant W. Langston, Samuel S. White 3rd and Vera White, with additional funds contributed by John Howard McFadden, Jr., Thomas Skelton Harrison, and the Philip H. and A.S.W. Rosenbach Foundation, 1985

1985-052-15920

Philadelphia, Pennsylvania

This German print illustrates the passage, "They sat down upon the ground with him seven days and seven nights, but none of them spoke a word to him: for they saw how great was his suffering" (Job 2:13). This work contains many elements common to other depictions of Job (wife in the background, broken pottery, destroyed buildings, and an undraped Job without sores). In this work, typical of nineteenth century romantic images, the emphasis shifts to Job himself rather than the conditions around him.

Stölzel and Jäger were contemporaries of the Nazarenes, a group of German artists who attempted to revive Christian art in the early nineteenth century. Jäger, an historic fresco and mural painter from the Leipsic and Dresden Academies, studied under Julius Schnorr, a member of the Nazarenes. The main subjects of Jäger's works were heroic and religious figures. This print was reproduced from a painting he completed in 1833.

25.

Job and His Friends

Date unknown
Paul Falconer Poole, artist
(1807-1879)
Herbert Bourne, engraver
(1820-1885)
Engraving
Special Collections F74.2.2
The Library of the Jewish
Theological Seminary of
America
New York City, New York

This highly romantic and allegorical image of Job is embellished with lush drapery, flowing costumes, and dramatic figures with arms outstretched and eyes fixed on the elixir being poured. A winged Satan appears in the background, although there is no sign of the suffering Job. The messenger in the center of the composition brings visual focus to his impending announcement. (Job 1:15)

Paul Falconer Poole, a genre English painter associated with the Bristol School, was known for his literary, historical, and biblical paintings. Although Poole was criticized for his clumsy drawing skills by some, he was admired by the Pre-Raphaelites, a group known for their zealous romanticism. Poole exhibited at the Royal Academy and was later elected to membership in 1861.

Herbert Bourne was an English engraver recognized for his work with the *Art Journal*, a periodical of aesthetic and literary criticism in the mid-1800s.

26.

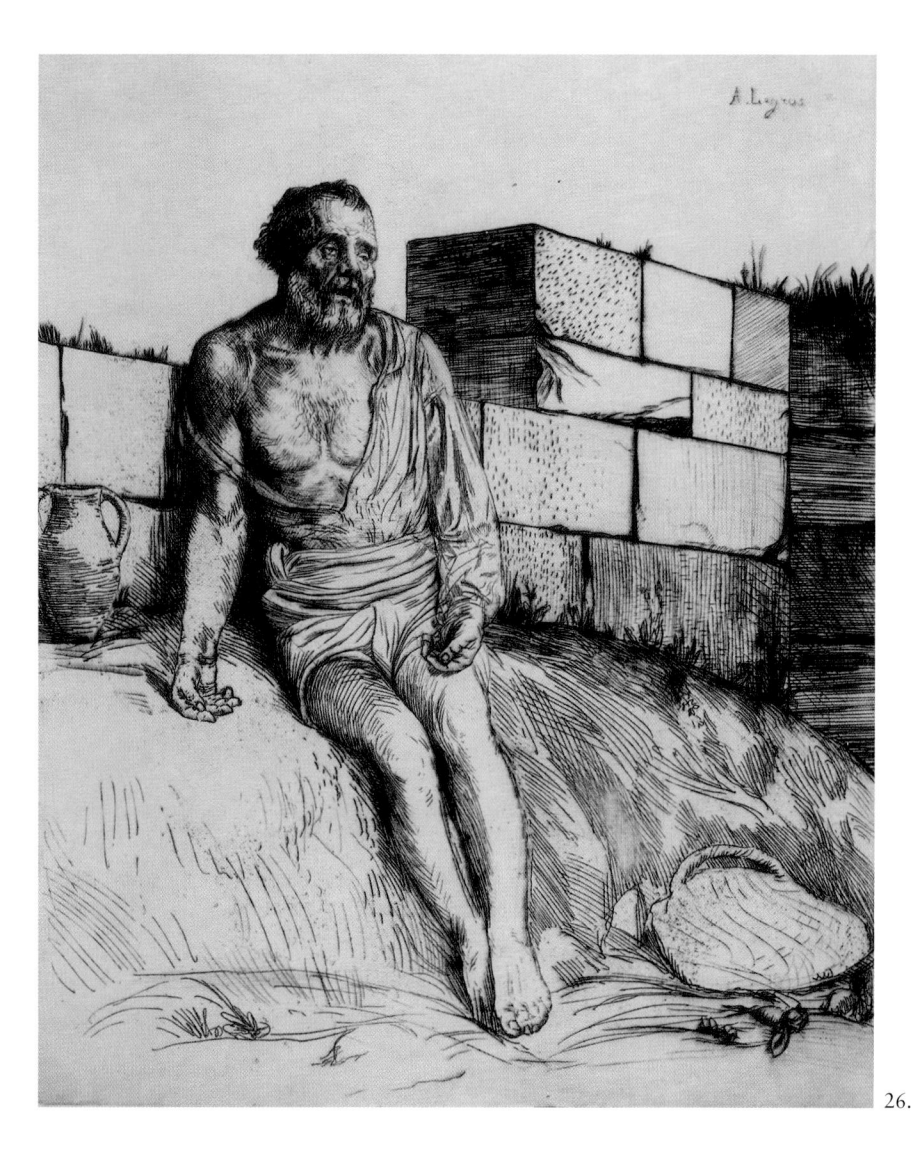

Job, 1st Plate

Date unknown
Alphonse Legros (1830-1911)
Drypoint and Etching
National Gallery of Art, Washington
Gift of George Matthews Adams in memory of his mother, Lydia Havens Adams
1952
1952.10.24 (B-17, 402B-19402)

This iconoclastic Job, the first of three etching states, is solitary, a singular Promethean character, a Job of desolation and despair.

Legros, a close friend of James McNeill Whistler and James Jacques Tissot, was instrumental in the revival of etching and engraving as an art form in England. Raised in poverty and neglect, Legros received little formal training in art, working instead as an apprentice to a building painter and later creating theatre sets. He successfully participated in the Salon at the Louvre in 1857 and in the Salon des Refusés in 1859. In spite of Degas' encouragement to join the Impressionist movement, Legros became a member of the Realist group headed by Courbet. Death had a tremendous appeal to Legros' imagination and his etchings included illustrations for the stories of Edgar Allen Poe, as well as landscapes, portraits, scenes of farm life, and religious figures.

James Jaques Tissot, a romantic Victorian painter known for his fashion-plate artistry, dedicated himself to illustrating the Bible following the untimely death of his mistress Kathleen Newton. Like many others of that period, he dabbled in seances and spiritualism, and eventually re-converted during the intense Catholic Revival that dominated France in the later part of the nineteenth century.

The Tissot Bible was highly popular and regarded with some jealousy by Tissot's peers, including his friend Edgar Degas. These illustrations enjoyed "block buster" success and eventually traveled to the Brooklyn Museum in New York City in 1894, bringing in the sum of $60,000. They also were exhibited at the Salon du Champ-de-Mars in 1901.

Although Tissot completed 95 of the illustrations, he never lived to see the publication of his series on the Hebrew Bible. Following his death, the illustrations were completed either from his sketches or in his style by his six studio assistants.

27.

Job and His Family

c. 1896-1902
James Jacques Joseph Tissot (1836-1902) and followers
Gouache on paper
The Jewish Museum,
New York
Gift of the heirs of Jacob Schiff
X1952-388
New York City, New York

This image of Job and his sons and daughters portrays his wealth and status as the family patriarch.

In an interview following Tissot's experiences in the Holy Land, he said that "a certain receptivity was induced in me which so intensified my powers of intuition, that the scenes of the past rose up before my mental vision in a peculiar and striking manner."

Job Hears Bad Tidings

c. 1896-1902
Studio of James Jacques
Joseph Tissot (1835-1902)
Gouache on paper
The Jewish Museum,
New York
Gift of the heirs of Jacob Schiff
X1952-389
New York City, New York

In this painting the messenger comes to give Job news of the disasters inflicted upon his children and servants. It shows the reaction to the biblical passage, "A messenger came to Job and said, 'The oxen were plowing and the donkeys were feeding beside them and the Sabeans fell on them…and killed the servants…a great wind came across, struck the four corners of the house and it fell on the young people'" (Job 1:13-19). Job looks concerned but calm while everyone else appears to grieve. The elegant background and richly colored garments provide an aristocratic and filtered view of his tragedy.

Job Lying on the Heap of Refuse

c. 1896-1902
Studio of James Jacques
Joseph Tissot (1835-1902)
Gouache on paper
The Jewish Museum,
New York
Gift of the heirs of Jacob Schiff
X1952-390
New York City, New York

Job lies on a cloth rather than a dungheap as suggested by the title. Where other backgrounds from this series are pastoral, this setting is more barren, including only broken pottery. It is interesting to note that the comforters' dress and hair color are rendered differently from another image of Job and his friends executed by the artist elsewhere in the same volume (cat. no. 29).

Job and His Three Friends

c.1896-1902
Studio of James Jacques
Joseph Tissot (1835-1902)
Gouache on paper
The Jewish Museum,
New York
Gift of the heirs of Jacob Schiff
X1952-391
New York City, New York

Job is illustrated in a romantic Oriental style and flanked with sympathetic comforters. The patrician Job suffers, but does so with dignity and elegance.

31.

Job Joins His Family in Happiness

c. 1896-1902
Studio of James Jacques
Joseph Tissot (1835-1902)
Gouache on paper
The Jewish Museum,
New York
Gift of the heirs of Jacob Schiff
X1952-392
New York City, New York

According to the biblical text, Job was restored two-fold and everyone who had known him before came and broke bread with him. This restoration scene suggests relief rather than joyous celebration.

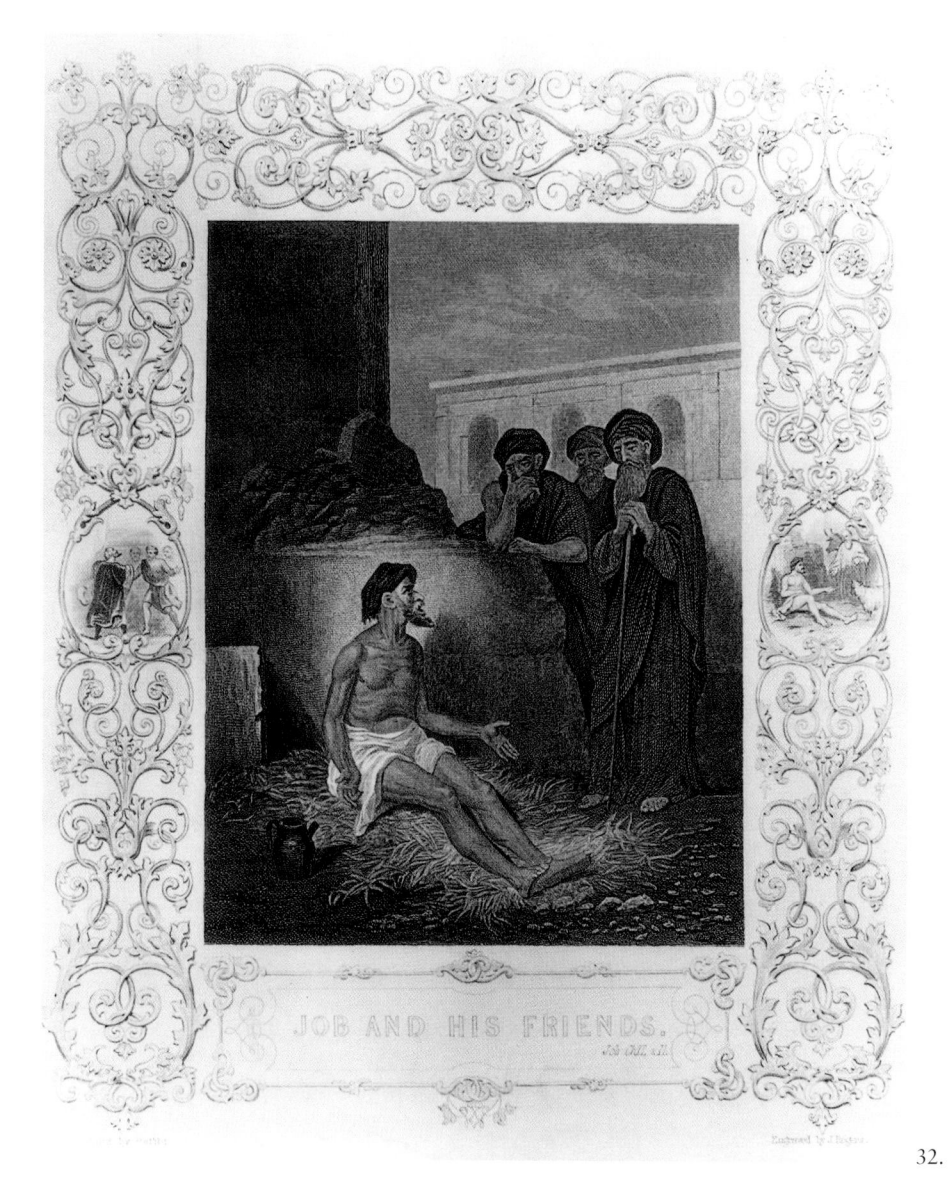

Job and His Friends

date unknown
John Rogers, Engraver (1808-1888?)
Denis Auguste Marie Raffet, Painter (1804-1860)
Engraving
Special Collections F74-2.7
The Library of the Jewish Theological Seminary of America
New York City, New York

This depiction of Job on a bundle of wheat is an older, more philosophical Job, and includes grand scale architectural elements, pottery, and the three comforters standing in silence. Two small illustrations in the margins render Job's suffering in a somewhat different style. A young, muscular Job is seated with outstretched arm accompanied by a lone comforter and some livestock. The other small marginal illustration depicts Job receiving news of his misfortunes from the messenger.

This engraving printed by the London Printing and Publishing Co. is created after a painting by Denis Auguste Marie Raffet, a French lithographer and illustrator. Raffet is best known for his illustrations of French history. The London Printing and Publishing Co., established in both London and New York, produced maps, Bibles, and fine prints.

33.

Job in Deep Distress

date unknown
Engraving
Special Collections F74-3.1
The Library of the Jewish Theological Seminary of America
New York City, New York

This very stylized book plate of Job has him seated on a hill scattered with grass, debris, and bones. The wife, dressed in period costume, points her hand toward the heavens. This muscular, patrician Job appears only to be inconvenienced by sores rather than truly suffering.

34.

Book of Job (Das Buch Hiob)
#24 of Limited Edition
1917
Willy Jaeckel (1888-1944)
Lithograph
The Jewish Museum
JM 30-68.1
New York City, New York

This illustration of Job and his family includes a Menorah, implying a parallel between the woes of Job and those of a Jewish family in Nazi Germany.

In 1937, The National Socialist Society for German Culture produced *Entartete Kunst* (degenerate art), a special exhibit organized by Nazi officials that purged German museums of 650 works considered to be degenerative to society. The purpose was to educate people about the relationship of art and race; modern art was commonly described as "Jewish," "degenerate," and "Bolshevik." This exhibition included works by Jaeckel, Chagall, Kandinsky, Grosz, Klee, Mondrian, and others.

Jaeckel was a German Expressionist painter and printmaker whose works brought him great recognition but were suppressed for their anti-war sentiments. *Das Buch Hiob* was followed by many illustrations of Dante and Goethe, and Jaeckel continued to work until he was drafted in World War I. Following the war he began to study religious, theosophical, and philosophical ideas, and received an appointment to the Staatliche Kunsthochschule, an academy of art in Berlin. Dismissed by the Nazis in 1933, he was reinstated after student protests. Jaeckel's studio was destroyed by bombs in 1943, and he died in a bombing raid in 1944.

Many American artists were assisted by the Federal Arts Project, a relief program set up by the Works Progress Administration (WPA) under President Franklin D. Roosevelt in 1935. This program employed artists for a variety of projects and supported sixteen Graphic Arts Division Workshops. The workshops employed over 250 artists, several of whom are represented in this catalogue.

35.

Figure of Job
1942

Ahron Ben-Shmuel

(1903-1984)

Bronze Sculpture

The Philadelphia Museum of Art: Gift of Mr. and Mrs. Benjamin Tepper, 1959

Philadelphia, Pennsylvania

This figure of Job looks Oriental, reflecting Ben-Shmuel's interest in primitive, Egyptian, and archaic Greek sculpture. Job is humbled, a singular, suffering man of endurance.

Ben-Shmuel was a WPA artist and Guggenheim Foundation Fellow known for his granite carvings. While in his teens he apprenticed with a stone cutter, and in the 1920s he began his own work.

36.

Job

1945
Ivan Mestrovic (1883-1962)
Bronze Maquette
20th Century Collection
Courtesy of Syracuse University Art Collection
Syracuse, New York

This expressive image of an iconoclastic Job is full of suffering and anguish. Job is no longer a man of patience, but rather a man of endurance.

Mestrovic taught himself to read at the age of 12 by comparing the written text of the Bible with the stories he'd heard his mother recite from memory. Inspired by the epic heroes and deeds, this Croatian sculptor carved figures in wood and stone, and later attended the Art Academy in Vienna. He was a close friend of Rodin and enjoyed a promising career with Picasso-like popularity before the war. Mestrovic was imprisoned briefly in 1941 and afterwards moved to the United States, where he taught at the University of Notre Dame in Indiana and Syracuse University. A prolific worker, Mestrovic created nearly 2000 sculptures that focused first on themes of national myths, and later chiefly on biblical subjects.

Benton Spruance, a Philadelphia resident, taught at the Pennsylvania Academy of Art and was influenced by Bellows, Dürer, Rembrant, Goya, and Blake.

The mythic vision of Job by this WPA artist stems from personal experiences and his reading of modern literature. Spruance spent much of his time exploring the human condition through his artwork. Considered one of the finest printmakers of the World War II period, Spruance used lithography as his primary medium. Ben Shahn, whose works appear in cat. nos. 45 and 46, once remarked that Spruance's images "expressed his sorrow and bitterness about the human capacity for endless war and violence."

37.

The Word and Job

1951

Benton Murdoch Spruance (1904-1967)

Woodcut

Philadelphia Museum of Art: Purchased with the Lola Downin Peck Fund from the Carl and Laura Zigrosser Collection, 1973

1973-012-186

Philadelphia, Pennsylvania

I Will Demand of Thee
(Synopsis of Job 38)

This confrontational image of Job includes God in the upper corner and refers to the voice from the whirlwind.

A WPA realist and artist, Spruance believed his artwork furthered social awareness and his cause. Only four woodcuts are known to have been created by Spruance, two of which are of Job. Initially, Spruance employed other printmakers to execute his work. After a friend encouraged him to follow in the footsteps of William Blake, Spruance embarked on making his own print of this work.

38.

Book of Job (or Jehovah and Satan)

1951

Benton Murdoch Spruance (1904-1967)

Color Woodcut

Philadelphia Museum of Art: Purchased with the Lola Downin Peck Fund from the Carl and Laura Zigrosser Collection, 1973.

1973-012-199

Philadelphia, Pennsylvania

This woodcut, also created in 1951, is a striking modernistic image of Job. The strong lines and contorted shapes create drama and tension as Job's faith is tested in the wager between God and Satan.

Ben-Zion was born in Stari Constantin, a large city in the western Ukraine. His father did not approve of either his studies at the Yeshiva or his interest in art, and Ben-Zion was forced to put the art aside. When the Cossacks invaded Galicia during the first World War, the family escaped to Vienna and then immigrated to America. For many years he earned his living by giving private Hebrew lessons. During this period Ben-Zion began to write poetry and to paint in earnest, portraying stories from the biblical texts he studied at the Yeshiva. He was disquieted by the rising fascism in Europe and racial injustice in the U.S. during the Great Depression. Commissions from the WPA offered Ben-Zion some financial relief and professional opportunity.

39.

Now when Job's three friends heard of all this evil that was come upon him, they came every one from his own place;—for they had made an appointment together to come to mourn with him and to comfort him. (Job II vs. 11)

From the portfolio *The Book of Ruth-Job-Song of Songs*, 1954
Ben-Zion (1897-1987), Etching
The Jewish Museum, New York
JM54-68.7

Job is seated, and the arms of the cropped comforters add visual impact to the composition. The supposed friends' accusatory fingers summarize their rounds of speeches, suggesting that Job or his children have sinned and he is not being punished enough.

Ben-Zion's etchings of Bible illustrations are an extension of the same images produced as oil paintings. Most of his biblical renderings are heroic in character and theme. This volume of the *Book of Ruth-Job-Song of Songs* was originally meant to be part of a cycle of four volumes on biblical themes. The first three volumes were published by Curt Valentin, whose death ended the publication of the fourth volume, *Judges and Kings*.

40.

But where shall wisdom be found? and where is the place of understanding? Job XXVIII, 12.

From the portfolio The Book of Ruth-Job-Song of Songs
1954
Ben-Zion (1897-1987)
Etching
The Jewish Museum, New York
JM54-68.10

Another plate from *The Book of Ruth, Job, Song of Songs* is of a Job in despair. The use of the over-sized hands bent toward God emphasizes the insistent questions Job asks God.

The heroes of the Hebrew Bible are frequent themes in Ben-Zion's work: Noah, Abraham, Jacob, Joseph, Ruth, and always Job and Moses. Through his artwork, Ben-Zion explores the possibility of dialogue between human beings and their creator.

41.

Illustration from *Job*

(The Book of Ruth, Job and Song of Songs)
1954
Ben-Zion (1897-1987)
Etching
Baltimore Museum of Art:
Purchase Fund
1956.165

Oh that I were as in months past, as in the days when God preserved me:
When his candle shined upon my head, and when by his light I walked through darkness; Job XXIX:2-3

In Job's final speeches he reaffirms his innocence, and he speaks of the divine protection he enjoyed earlier in his life. Job has reconciled himself to his state of misery and recites a litany of confessions to question his plight before God. This image of Job reconciled shows his submission to the situation, which he has ceased to resist.

42.

The Book of Job

1955
Fritz Eichenberg (1901-1990)
Wood Engraving (trial proof)
National Gallery of Art,
Washington, Rosenwald
Collection 1980
19980. 45.463 (B-32502)

This print is one of ten wood engravings commissioned as illustrations for the *Catholic Worker*. The engraving conveys the comforters' amazement over Job's situation. The angel of death looms in the background, with the eye of God overhead, while the comforters sit on mats looking on in wonder. As is typical of this period, Job displays no sores, nor is his wife included.

In the twentieth century, with World War II and the modern technology that accompanied it, came the birth of a new, politically and socially conscious image of Job. Social realists such as Fritz Eichenberg, Misch Kohn, Ben Shahn, and Benton Spruance all used Job as an iconoclastic figure in their new awareness of destruction and vulnerability.

Eichenberg was born in Germany of Jewish parents. His father's death of Parkinson's disease when Eichenberg was 14 added to his growing awareness of mortality, which was accompanied by his distaste for Hitler's Germany. Eichenberg was influenced and inspired by Hogarth, Bosch, Goya, and Daumier—all artists who contributed to his growing sense of social responsibility. Eichenberg was a great admirer of Dostoyevsky, Tolstoy, Gorky, Dickens, and Kafka, and created illustrations for some of their works.

In 1933, Eichenberg left Germany to escape Hitler and moved to New York where he worked for the Works Progress Administration. He returned to Germany to retrieve his wife and she died not long after her arrival in the U.S. In 1949 Eichenberg met Dorothy Day, the publisher of the *Catholic Worker*, for which he provided many images.

43.

Job Reconciled
1957
Ben-Zion (1897-1987)
Oil
Ben-Zion Collection
New York City, New York

The Book of Job was a recurring theme for Ben-Zion, appearing in sketches, prints, and paintings throughout his life. This painting recalls a 1954 etching from *The Book of Ruth-Job-Song of Songs*.

89

44.

Job

1959
Misch Kohn (b.1916-)
Woodcut
Prints & Photographs Division
Library of Congress,
Washington, D.C.
LCUSZ62-43306

This image of Job presents a haunting reminder of the Holocaust. Job stand with his arms circled about his head, creating the shape a nuclear mushroom cloud.

Kohn, born in Indiana to Jewish Russian immigrant parents, was a socially conscious artist whose works focused on heroic images. While at the WPA, Kohn produced color lithographs and small wood engravings with a strong political message. His images are very different from the others in this exhibition, with their use of strong lines and sense of movement. Kohn is known for his technical expertise and experimentation with color in furthering the limits of the printmaking process.

Ben Shahn was born in Lithuania, the eldest of five children in an Orthodox Jewish family. Shahn's father, an active socialist, worked as a wood carver before he was exiled to Siberia. The family immigrated to America, where at the age of 14 Shahn apprenticed to a lithographer. He was concerned about the specters of poverty, nuclear holocaust, and the potential dangers of technology. Like other Social Realists, Shahn was an artistic Robin Hood who dedicated his art to dignifying the plight of the poor and assaulting the conscience of the rich. Shahn first worked for the WPA as an artist and photographer, documenting poverty in rural America. Later he was blacklisted by the House Un-American Activities Committee during the Cold War.

45.

Pleiades

1960
Ben Shahn (1898-1967)
Lithograph
Prints and Photographs Division
Library of Congress, Washington, D.C.
XXS526D13

Can you bind the chains of the Pleiades, or loose the cords of Orion? Can you lead forth the Mazzaroth in their season? Do you know the ordinances of the heavens? Can you establish their rule on the earth? Can you lift up your voice to the clouds, that a flood of waters may cover you? Can you send forth lightnings, that they may go and say to you, 'here we are'?
(Job 38:31-36, in Hebrew)

The title of this lithograph is a reference to God's stern speech to Job, intended to put him in his place, with its reference to the creation of the heavens. Speaking of this print, Shahn once remarked that "whereas scientists present their own theories regarding the origins of life, when Job was unconsoled he challenged God himself."

Shahn was fascinated with script from his early childhood and used lettering as an important part of many of his compositions. Shahn created several Job-related works in paintings and prints, including the mask designs of Satan and God for Archibald MacLeish's 1959 play, *J.B.*

Where Wast Thou?

1964
Ben Shahn (1898-1967)
Gouache and Gold Leaf on paper mounted on masonite
Amon Carter Museum,
Fort Worth, Texas
1967.198

Where were you when I laid the foundations of the earth? Tell me, if you have understanding. Who determined its measurements—surely you know! Or who stretched the line upon it?
On what were its bases sunk, or who laid its cornerstone,
When the morning stars sang together, and all the sons of God shouted for joy?
(Job 38:4-7, in Hebrew)

The rebellious Shahn uses the Job imagery to address injustice, in a response to the horrors of World War II.

47.

Book of Job, The Leviathan (or The Blue Whale)

No. 16 from the series *Moby Dick: The Passion of Ahab*
1966, Lithograph
Benton Murdoch Spruance
(1904-1967)
Philadelphia Museum of Art:
Gift of an anonymous donor.
1972
1972-070-001

While Ben Shahn through his images uses the voice of God to remind Job of his place in the universe, here it is Spruance who questions God. This lithograph appeared in an edition of *Moby Dick*, but refers to the biblical passage where God speaks to Job, saying "Can you lead about Leviathan with a hook, or curb his tongue with a bit?" (Job 40:25). In the Bible, the leviathan is a symbol of the power and goodness of God. For Melville and Spruance, it is a representation of the divine's unfathomable nature and perhaps malevolence.

Spruance spent the last several years of his life creating images for *Moby Dick*—sometimes interpreted as the contemporary literary parallel of the Book of Job—and planned for its printing posthumously. These illustrations were not meant to illustrate the epic, but rather to offer commentary on the philosophical nuances. Religious subjects (Jacob, Tobias, Job, and Lamentations) and myths were predominant themes in his work until his death in 1967.

48.

After Blake's Job

1966
Lithograph in black and gray on Rives BFK paper (proof)
Benton Murdoch Spruance (1904-1967)
National Gallery of Art, Washington, Rosenwald Collection

The scene of the restoration of Job and his family mirrors the composition created by Blake. The tree is located in the center with sons and daughters on each side, Job is playing a harp, his children are holding trumpets and harps, and a moon appears in the left hand corner. Spruance has also included mythological figures around the border, and sheep in the foreground.

Spruance was an admirer of Blake, who spent the latter years of his life illustrating the Book of Job. In connecting his images of Job with the written word, Spruance's print is a tribute to both Blake and the human condition.

Spruance was not a conventional religious man. Biblical events were significant to him for what they had to say about the unfolding of the human drama and about man's capacity for both good and evil.

49.

Job: A Comedy of Justice

1984
Michael Whelan (b.1950 -)
Acrylic
The Kelly Collection of American Illustration

Job is surrounded by modern gadgets, perhaps symbolizing the temptation of riches rather than the loss of worldly goods.

Job continued to be used in the late twentieth century as an icon for injustice and suffering. *Job: A Comedy of Justice*, authored by science fiction writer Robert A. Heinlein, is a contemporary tale of a minister who suffers a series of trials, with all signs pointing to Armageddon and the Day of Judgement.

The Book of Mechtilde

This contemporary 40-page illuminated manuscript based on *The Book of Job* tells the story of the artist's mother, Sheila Mechtilde Henriques, and her battle with cancer. A former Miss Jamaica and mother of three, Mechtilde's plight is described through narrative prose, poetry, and illuminations. Flora and fauna native to the Caribbean and representations of Mechtilde's Jewish heritage surround the central illustration and text for each page. This autobiographical volume is a personal homage to Mechtilde and serves as a catharsis for her grieving daughter who confronts the issues of life, unjust suffering, and death.

50.

Leaf from *The Book of Mechtilde*

1992

Anna Ruth Henriques (b.1967 -)

Ink, gouache, and paint on paper

Museum Purchase with funds provided by The Reed Foundation, the Fine Arts Acquisition Committee, and the United Congregation of Israelites—Jewish Community of Jamaica, West Indies

The Jewish Museum, New York

The opening verse of Henriques' book echoes the initial lines of Job, "In the Land of Jah, there lived a good woman named Mechtilde…" and accompanies the illustration which cites the prologue of Job. In the tradition of the illuminated Renaissance manuscripts, Henriques has included a foliated border of native plants. The center illustration portrays Mechtilde with one of her babies, above the watchful eye of God.

51.

Leaf from *The Book of Mechtilde*

1992

Anna Ruth Henriques (b.1967 -)

Ink, gouache, and paint on paper

Museum Purchase with funds provided by The Reed Foundation, the Fine Arts Acquisition Committee, and the United Congregation of Israelites—Jewish Community of Jamaica, West Indies

The Jewish Museum, New York

Why has not Shaddai his own store of times, and why do his faithful never see his days?...
(Job 24:1-5)

Mechtilde, who has not yet lost her hair, is in the center of the illustration surrounded by a foliated border including tree limbs, snakes, and an apple above her head. The tree in early Christian symbolism indicates the tree of knowledge.

In the biblical citation contained in the illustration, Job complains about the deeds of the wicked and how they escape punishment.

52.

Leaf from *The Book of Mechtilde*

1992

Anna Ruth Henriques (b.1967 -)

Ink, gouache, and paint on paper

Museum Purchase with funds provided by The Reed Foundation, the Fine Arts Acquisition Committee, and the United Congregation of Israelites—Jewish Community of Jamaica, West Indies

The Jewish Museum, New York

As God liveth, who taken away my right, and the Almighty who hath dealt bitterly with me; all the while my breath is in me...
(Job 27:1-23)

Mechtilde is in the boat while her three daughters watch from the shore.

Job reaffirms his innocence in this passage, one of the most vitriolic in the Bible.

53.

Leaf from *The Book of Mechtilde*

1992

Anna Ruth Henriques (b.1967 -)

Ink, gouache, and paint on paper

Museum Purchase with funds provided by The Reed Foundation, the Fine Arts Acquisition Committee, and the United Congregation of Israelites—Jewish Community of Jamaica, West Indies

The Jewish Museum, New York

Why did I not die at birth...?
(Job 3:1-16)

The ailing Mechtilde is shown suffering the side effects of her medical treatments, and by now has lost her hair. The eye of God is centered at the top and bottom of the page. Apples provide marginal borders; in the Christian tradition they are considered to be an allusion to Eve, and thus emblems both of sin and salvation. This lament of innocent suffering from a contemporary woman echoes Job's initial cry that he suffers undeservedly.

Sources and Further Reading

For a general introduction to the history and terminology used for illuminated manuscripts, see Michelle Brown, *Understanding Illuminated Manuscripts, A Guide to Technical Terms,* The J. Paul Getty Museum in association with The British Library, (Malibu, CA Christopher Hudson, Publisher, 1994), and Janet Backhouse, *The Iluminated Manuscript,* Phaidon Press Limited, (Oxford, 1979), pp.8-10.

Information on symbols and their meanings used in Christian art can be found in the book by George Ferguson, *Signs & Symbols in Christian Art,* Oxford University Press, 1975. The connection between the early illuminated manuscripts, the William Blake works, and the Henriques contemporary illuminated manuscript is more easily defined with the use of this volume.

For specific information on the *Icones Historarium,* see Oskar Batschmann, and Pascal Greiner, *Hans Holbein,* Princeton University Press, (Princeton, 1977), pp. 60-63. The life of Holbein as an English court painter and his political and philosophical sentiments are discussed. The website for Octavo Editions: (http://www.octavo.com/collections/projects/hlbtst/about) offers a commentary by Erika Michael.

On the history of the art of printing, refer to Christopher Barth and Anne Quinn, *The Infancy of Printing, Incunabula at the Golda Meir Library* (http://www.uwm.edu/Dept/Library/special/exhibits/incunab/incpg18.html).

The influence of the Reformation on German artist Giulia Bartrum is found in *German Renaissance Prints 1490-1550,* British Museum Press, (London, 1995), pp. 99-100 and pp.183-210. *The Grove Dictionary of Art, 2002* (www.artnet.com) offers notes on peasant uprisings and the views of Martin Luther, as they pertain to Beham and Hirschvogel.

For more information on the history of Dutch artists refer to the exhibition catalogue by Barbara Butts and Joseph Leo Koerner, *The Printed World of Pieter Bruegel the Elder,* The St. Louis Art Museum, 1995, and the volume by Ilja M. Veldman, Ger Juijten, ed. *The Dutch & Flemish Etchings, Engravings and Woodcuts 1450-1700,* (Roosendaal: Koninklijke Van Poll, 1993), p.140. Also, Veldman's essay in the *Grove Dictionary of Art,* Volumes 15 and 17, ed. Jane Turner, Macmillan Publishers Limited (New York, 1996) offers biographical information on Coornhert and Heemskerck.

On Peter Paul Rubens' works, see Julius S. Held, *Rubens Selected Drawings With an Introduction and Critical Catalogue, Vol. I, The Text,* The Phaidon Press Ltd., (London, 1959), p.130 and Bolton Museum, Art Gallery & Aquarium (http://www.boltonmuseums.org.uk/rubens2.htm) for background on Rubens and his workshop engravers.

A general reference for the background of Mitelli can be found in the book by Marcus S. Sophar with Claudia Lazzaro-Bruns, *Seventeenth Century Italian Prints,* Cardinal Co. (San Francisco: 1978), p. 52. and Bartleby.com Great Books online (http://www.bartleby.com/65/re/Reni-Gui.html). For information on Reni, see the essay by Richard E. Spear in Vol. 26, *Grove Dictionary of Art,* ed. Jane Turner, 1996, Macmillan Publishers Limited (New York: 1996), p.195-204.

An essay on the life and work of Le Vilain is located in the work by John Denison Champlin, Jr., and Charles C. Perkins, eds. *Cyclopedia of Painters and Paintings.* Volume II, Empire State Book Co. 1927. Fra Bartolommeo's life and work is included in Ludovico Borgo's and Margot Borgo's essay in Vol. 3 Grove Dictionary of Art, ed. Jane Turner, 1996, Macmillan Publishers Limited, (New York: 1996), p.302-306.

Samuel Terrien's work, *The Iconography of Job Through the Centuries, Artists as Biblical Interpreters,* The Pennsylvania State University Press, (University Park: 1996), p.195, provides resources for early Job iconography.

Blake's interpretative history can be found in Meira Perry-Lehman, ed. *There Was a Man in the Land of Uz,* "From Sketch to Print: on the Evolution of Blake's Illustrations to the Book of Job" by Meira Perry-Lehman, and "Blake's Vision as Reflected in His Engraving to the Book of Job," by Miriam Orr, Sabinsky Press Ltd., (Tel Aviv: 1992), pp.37-38 and 58. For specific information on the *Book of Job* see David Bindman, *William Blake His Art and His Time,* Thames and Hudson, Ltd. (London: 1982), p.174. and Joseph H. Wicksteed, *Blake's Vision of The Book of Job,* Haskell House Publishers Ltd., (New York: 1971), pp. 67, 97.

Refer to John Denison Champlin, Jr. ed., *Cyclopedia of Painters and Paintings,* Vol. II, Empire State Book Co., (New York: 1927), p.330 for outline of the works of Jäger.

On Poole's works, see Julian Treuherz essay in Vol. 25 *Grove Dictionary of Art*, ed. Jane Turner, 1996, Macmillan Publishers Limited, (New York: 1996), p.228. Bourne, the engraver of Poole's work was an English engraver based in London. His work is listed with Bruce A. Scharlau, *Scharlau Prints & Maps*, 2002.

On the relationship of Legros and his role in the revival of etching in England, see Walter Shaw Sparrow, *A Book of British Etching from Barlow to Seymour Haden*, John Lane the Bodley Head Limited, (London: 1926), p.68. A transcribed lecture and catalogue of his works is found in Harold James Lean Wright, *The Etchings, Drypoints and Lithographs of Alphonse Legros 1837-1911*, The Print Collector's Club, (London: 1934), p.10-15.

Tissot's in-depth biography and work as a Bible illustrator is included in Michael Wentworth's *James Tissot*, Oxford University Press (New York: 1984), pp.187-188 and Christopher Wood's *Tissot*, George Weidenfeld and Nicolson Ltd., (London: 1986), pp.15, 147-154.

On Raffet, see *The Columbia Encyclopedia, Fifth Edition*, Columbia University Press, 1994 and Athena S.E. Leoussi's essay in Vol. 25, *Grove Dictionary of Art*, ed. Jane Turner, 1996, Macmillan Publishers Limited, (New York: 1996), p.849.

For a general introduction to Fritz Eichenberg, see Robert Ellsberg, ed., *Fritz Eichenberg Works of Mercy*, (New York: Maryknoll, 1992), p.15; and the exhibition catalogue by Robert Conway, *Witness to Our Century, An Artistic Biography of Fritz Eichenberg*, Vanderbilt University, 1999, n.p.

Biographical information on Willy Jaeckel is located in Peter W. Guenther's essay in Vol. 16, *Grove Dictionary of Art*, ed. Jane Turner, 1996, Macmillan Publishers Limited, (New York: 1996). Degenerative Art (Entartete Kunst) is discussed in *The Teacher's Guide to the Holocaust* in the website: http://fcit.coedu.usf.edu/holocaust/arts/artDegen.htm; Essay by Jennifer McAllister, *The Degenerate Art Exhibit at the Munich Haus der Kunst*, (http:nimbus.ocis.temple.edu/~jlockeno/150/hdk.html).

An outline history of the Federal Arts Project: Graphic Arts Division is found in *The Ken Trevey Collection of American Realist Prints*, http://ucsbuxa.ucsb.edu/slide-collection/trevey/ trevey.html.

Information on the works of Ahron Ben-Shmuel is included in Volume 3 of *Who Was Who in American Art: 400 Years of Artists in America, 1564-1975*, Peter Hastings Falk, editor in chief and Audrey Lewis, head of research, 1999, Sound View Press, (Madison, CT). p.275.

The life and work of Mestrovic appear in Jure Mikuz's essay in Vol. 21 *Grove Dictionary of Art*, ed. Jane Turner, 1996, Macmillan Publishers Limited, (New York: 1996). Mestrovic's daughter, Maria Mestrovic has written an essay for Croatia Net (http://www.archaeology.net/croatia/html/mestrovic.html).

On the complete works of Spruance, see Ruth E. Fine and Robert F. Looney, *Benton Murdock Spruance, A Catalgoue Raisonné*, The University of Pennsylvania Press (University Park: 1986), p.3. Biographical information can be found in Lloyd M. Abernathy, *Benton Spruance: The Artist and the Man*, Art Alliance Press and Associated University Presses (Cranbury: 1988).

Ben-Zion's art work and writings are discussed in Duveen-Graham's exhibition catalogue *The Second and Third Portfolios of Biblical Etchings by Ben-Zion*, 1956; Essays by Tabita Shalem, Joseph Solman and Ori Z. Soltes, *Ben-Zion: In Search of Oneself*, B'nai B'rith Klutznick National Jewish Museum, 1977; *Prophets, Eighteen etchings: Ben-Zion*, essay by Ben-Zion, n.d.; and in the exhibition catalogue essay by Ben-Zion, *Ben-Zion Etchings on Biblical Themes*, Bezalel National Museum, Jerusalem, 1957.

A volume on the work of Misch Kohn is authored by Jo Farb Hernandez, *Misch Kohn Beyond the Tradition*, Monterey Museum of Art (Monterey: 1997), p.74.

Regarding Shahn's role as a "Robin Hood," I have referred to *300 Years of American Art, Vol. II* compiled by Michael David Zellman, The Wellfleet Press, Chelsea House Educational Communications, Inc., (Seacaucus: 1987), p. 878. Ben Shahn's political views and works is located in the essay "Ben Shahn in Postwar American Art Shared Visions" by Stephen Polcari, Susan Chevlowe, *Common Man, Mystic Vision: The Paintings of Ben Shahn*, The Princeton University Press, (Princeton: 1998), p.83. Shahn's quote regarding *Pleiades* is quoted from Kenneth W. Prescott, *Prints and Posters of Ben Shahn*, Dover Publications, Inc., (New York: 1982), p.24.

Photography Credits

Holbein Bible, Italian Bible, Byzantine Leaf Psalter, The Walters Art Museum, Baltimore.

Job: A Comedy of Justice, 1984, Michael Whelan, The Kelly Collection of American Illustration.

Job and his Friends F74.2.7, *Job in Deep Distress*, F74.3.1, *Job and his Friends*, F74.2.2, Courtesy of the Library of the Jewish Theological Seminary of America.

Where Wast Thou? Amon Carter Museum, Fort Worth, Texas.

Job, Syracuse University Art Collection.

The Triumph of Job, Maerten van Heemskerck, Gift of Walter H. and Leonore Annenberg in Honor of the 50th Anniversary of the National Gallery of Art 1990, 1990.47.3./DR, Photograph © Board of Trustees, National Gallery of Art, Washington.

Triumph of Job, Dirck Volckertz Coornhert after Maerten van Heemskerck, Ailsa Mellon Bruce Fund 1974, 1974.53.9.(B-27300)/PR, Photograph © Board of Trustees, National Gallery of Art, Washington.

Job Learns of His Misfortunes, Augustin Hirschvogel, Rosenwald Collection 1950, 1950.17.194.(B-19051)/PR, Photograph © Board of Trustees, National Gallery of Art, Washington.

Satan Before the Throne of God, William Blake, Gift of W.G. Russell Allen, 1941 1941.1.227. (B-247)/PR Photograph © Board of Trustees, National Gallery of Art, Washington.

Satan Smiting Job with Boils, William Blake, Gift of W.G. Russell Allen, 1941, 1941.1.231.(B-251)/PR, Photograph © Board of Trustees, National Gallery of Art, Washington.

The Lord Answering Job Out of the Whirlwind, William Blake, Gift of W.G. Russell Allen, 1941, 1941. 1. 238.(B-258)/PR, Photograph © Board of Trustees, National Gallery of Art, Washington.

Job's Sacrifice, William Blake, Gift of W.G. Russell Allen, 1941, 1941.1.243.(B-263)/PR, Photograph © Board of Trustees, National Gallery of Art, Washington.

Job and His Daughters, William Blake Gift of W.G. Russell Allen, 1941, 1941.1. 245.(B-265)/PR, Photograph © Board of Trustees, National Gallery of Art, Washington.

Job and His Wife Restored to Posterity, William Blake, Gift of W.G. Russell Allen, 1941, 1941.1.246.(B-266)/PR, Photograph © Board of Trustees, National Gallery of Art, Washington.

Job 1st Plate, Alphonse Legros, Gift of George Matthews Adams in memory of his mother, Lydia Havens Adams 1952, 1952.10.24 (B-20141), Photograph © Board of Trustees, National Gallery of Art, Washington

After Blake's Job, Benton Murdoch Spruance (1904-1967), Rosenwald Collection, (1980.45.1372), Photograph © Board of Trustees, National Gallery of Art, Washington.

The Book of Job, Fritz Eichenberg, Rosenwald Collection 1980, 19980. 45.463(B-32502)/PR, Photograph © Board of Trustees, National Gallery of Art, Washington.

Book of Hours, 1400, Rare Book and Special Collections Division, Library of Congress, Washington, D.C.

Bible, German, Anton Koberger, Lessing J. Rosenwald Collection, Rare Book & Special Collections Division, The Library of Congress, Washington, D.C.

Book of Hours, 1524, Rosenwald Manuscript, Lessing J. Rosenwald Collection, Rare Book and Special Collections Division, The Library of Congress, Washington, D.C.

Biblisch Historien, figürlich fürgebiblet, Hans Sebald Beham, Lessing J. Rosenwald Collection, Rare Book of Special Collections Division, Library of Congress, Washington, D.C.

A Curious Hieroglyphic Bible, or, Select passages in the Old and New Testaments, represented with emblematical figures, for the amusement of youth: designed chiefly to familiarize tender age, in a pleasing and diverting manner, with early ideas of the Holy Scriptures: to which are subjoined, a short account of the lives of the Evangelists, and other pieces, illustrated with cuts, Rare Book & Special Collections Division, Library of Congress, Washington, D.C.

Job, Misch Kohn, Prints & Photographs Division, Library of Congress, Washington, D.C.

Pleiades, Ben Shahn, Prints and Photographs Division, Library of Congress, Washington, D.C.

Job Reconciled, Ben-Zion, Ben-Zion Collection.

Qisas al-Anbiya (Legends of the Prophets), Spencer Collection, The New York Public Library, Astor, Lenox and Tilden Foundations.

Illustration from "Job," 1954, Ben-Zion (1897-1987), Etching, 17⅝" x 13¾" Baltimore Museum of Art: Purchase Fund, 1956.165

"Job" after Fra Bartolommeo, Date unknown, Gerard Rene Le Vilain, French (1740-1836), Engraving, Baltimore Museum of Art: Garrett Collection, BMA 1946.112.3155.

Job and His Family, c. 1896-1902, James Jacques Joseph Tissot (1836-1902) and followers, Gift of the heirs of Jacob Schiff, ©The Jewish Museum, New York, Photo by Richard Goodbody.

Job Hears Bad Tidings, c. 1896-1902, Studio of James Jacques Joseph Tissot (1835-1902), Gift of the heirs of Jacob Schiff, ©The Jewish Museum, New York, Photo by Richard Goodbody.

Job and His Three Friends, c. 1896-1902, Studio of James Jacques Joseph Tissot (1835-1902), Gift of the heirs of Jacob Schiff, ©The Jewish Museum, New York, Photo by Richard Goodbody.

Job Lying on the Heap of Refuse, c. 1896-1902, Studio of James Jacques Joseph Tissot (1835-1902), Gift of the heirs of Jacob Schiff, ©The Jewish Museum, New York, Photo by Richard Goodbody.

Job Joins His Family in Happiness, c. 1896-1902, Studio of James Jacques Joseph Tissot (1835-1902), Gift of the heirs of Jacob Schiff, ©The Jewish Museum, New York, Photo by Richard Goodbody.

Book of Job (Das Buch Hiob) #24 of Limited Edition, 1917, Willy Jaeckel (1888-1944), ©The Jewish Museum, New York.

Now when Job's three friends heard of all this evil that was come upon him, they came every one from his own place;—for they had made an appointment to come to mourn with him and to comfort him. Job II: 11 From the portfolio The Book of Ruth-Job-Song of Songs, 1954, Ben-Zion (1897-1987), ©The Jewish Museum, New York.

But where shall wisdom be found? and where is the place of understanding? Job, XXVI-II, 12, From the portfolio The Book of Ruth-Job-Song of Songs, 1954, Ben-Zion (1897-1987), ©The Jewish Museum, New York.

The Book of Mechtilde, 1992, Anna Ruth Henriques (b.1967 -), 1999-84f, 84ddd, 84 ppp, 84fw. Museum Purchase with funds provided by The Reed Foundation, the Fine Arts Acquisition Committee, and the United Congregation of Israelites – Jewish Community of Jamaica, West Indies, ©The Jewish Museum, New York, printed with permission from Anna Ruth Henriques.

Job Tormented by Demons and Abused by his Wife, Vorsterman after Rubens, 1985-52-9972, Philadelphia Museum of Art.

Job, Christian Ernst Stölzel, 1985-52-15920, Philadelphia Museum of Art: The Muriel and Philip Berman gift, acquired from the John S. Philips Bequest of 1876 to the Pennsylvania Academy of Art.

The Word and Job, Benton Murdoch Spruance, 1973-12-186, Philadelphia Museum of Art: Purchased: Lola Downin Peck Fund.

Book of Job, Benton Murdoch Spruance, 1973-12-199, Philadelphia Museum of Art: Purchased: Lola Downin Peck Fund from the Carl and Laura Zigrosser Collection, 1973.

Book of Job, The Leviathan, Benton Murdoch Spruance, 1972-70-1, Philadelphia Museum of Art: Gift of an anonymous donor.

Figure of Job, Ahron Ben-Shmuel, 1959-124-1, Philadelphia Museum of Art: Gift of Mr. and Mrs. Benjamin Tepper, 1959.

Triumph of Job, Giusepe Mitelli, 1985-52-32658, Philadelphia Museum of Art: The Muriel and Philip Berman gift, acquired from the John S. Phillips bequest of 1876, The Philadelphia Academy of Art, 1985.

Job on the Dung Hill, Surrounded by his Friends and Wife, Anonymous after Rubens, 1985-52-42499, The Muriel and Philip Berman gift, acquired from the John S. Phillips bequest of 1876, The Philadelphia Academy of Art, 1985.

Job Conversing with his Friends, Hans Sebald Beham, 1985-52-33453, The Muriel and Philip Berman gift, acquired from the John S. Phillips bequest of 1876, The Philadelphia Academy of Art, 1985.

Artists

al-Nishapuri
Beham, Hans Sebald
Ben-Shmuel, Ahron
Ben-Zion
Blake, William
Bourne, Herbert
Coornhert, Dirck Volckertz
Eichenberg, Fritz
Heemskerck, Maerten van
Henriques, Anna Ruth
Hirschvogel, Augustin
Holbein, Hans (ii)
Jäger, Gustav Marie
Jaeckel, Willy
Koberger, Anton
Kohn, Misch
Legros, Alphonse
Le Vilain, Gerard Rene
Mestrovic, Ivan
Mitelli, Giuseppe Maria
Poole, Paul Falconer
Raffet, Denis Auguste Marie
Reni, Guido
Rogers, John
Rubens, Peter Paul
Shahn, Ben
Spruance, Benton Murdoch
Stölzel, Christian Ernst
Tissot, James Jacques Joseph
Vorsterman, Lucas (I)
Whelan, Michael